T0019585

By the same author

Fifteen Things They Forgot to Tell You About Autism
The Stuff that Transformed My Life as an Autism Parent
Debby Elley
ISBN 978 1 78592 438 5
eISBN 978 1 78450 810 4

Spectrum Women – Autism and Parenting
Renata Jurkevythz, Lisa Morgan and Maura Campbell
Foreword by Barb Cook
ISBN 978 1 78775 294 8
eISBN 978 1 78775 295 5

The Ice-Cream Sundae Guide to Autism
An Interactive Kids' Book for Understanding Autism
Debby Elley and Tori Houghton
ISBN 978 1 78775 380 8
eISBN 978 1 78775 381 5

Championing Your Autistic Teen at Secondary School
Getting the Best from Mainstream Settings
Debby Elley and Gareth D Morewood
ISBN 978 1 83997 074 0
eISBN 978 1 83997 075 7

JUST *the* JOB!

A Light-Hearted Guide to Office Life for the Autistic Employee

DEBBY ELLEY & MAURA CAMPBELL

(WHO HAVE BOTH WORKED IN LOADS OF OFFICES BY THE WAY)

Foreword by Sharon Didrichsen | Illustrated by Tim Stringer

Jessica Kingsley Publishers
London and Philadelphia

First published in Great Britain in 2024 by Jessica Kingsley Publishers
An imprint of John Murray Press

2

A CIP catalogue record for this title is available from the
British Library and the Library of Congress

ISBN 978 1 80501 248 1
eISBN 978 1 80501249 8

Printed and bound in the United States by Integrated Books International

Jessica Kingsley Publishers' policy is to use papers that are natural,
renewable and recyclable products and made from wood grown in
sustainable forests. The logging and manufacturing processes are expected
to conform to the environmental regulations of the country of origin.

Jessica Kingsley Publishers
Carmelite House
50 Victoria Embankment
London EC4Y 0DZ

www.jkp.com

John Murray Press
Part of Hodder & Stoughton Limited
An Hachette UK Company

CONTENTS

FOREWORD

I feel very privileged to write a foreword to this wonderful book. It's wonderful as it brings a sense of lightness to the serious task of getting and keeping a career. I have spent the last ten years supporting autistic and neurodivergent people to secure and progress in careers, sometimes with astounding results, along with our team at Specialisterne NI, our autistic and neurodivergent community, and employers. You may not think that the road has been paved with fun and laughter, but it has. It could be something about living in Northern Ireland or the shared humour (at times razor sharp) of some of our autistic community, but we have found that laughter helps, even in the face of obstacles in our way.

In my ten years I have noticed what helps autistic people feel better about themselves, more confident and more able to see work cultures for what they are. Rather than asking 'Why can't I fit in?' they decide how they can work at their best, which may involve not attending the work social (or attending all the work socials!), not looking at an interviewer or bringing a fidget to work. When I start to see that, I know I can pull back on support (although I may be asked to do a little bit of training so that a manager or peer understands more about autistic culture). I remember when I first referred to autism as a 'culture' with the autistic community at Specialisterne NI. I was greeted by silence, and ponderous looks. 'It's not a culture, it's a sub-culture', one of our community replied.

I think (my memory is not the best!) we went on to discuss how being autistic you interact with the culture you find yourself in. I would add that culture could be the culture and practices of the country you live in, the street where you grew up, the company you are applying to or the company or team in the company you work in. Which would explain why some people I have supported have been on the point of losing their job in one team, and all problems have been miraculously solved when they moved to a new team (as it had a better culture).

Here Maura and Debby are anthropologists, exploring the culture of work. You will learn not only from the content but also from the approach. Only this week I was speaking with someone who was attempting to recover from spending too long in a work culture which did not celebrate or acknowledge autistic ways of being. They asked me how they could maintain eye contact at interview, as when they did, their words disappeared from their mind.

Together we explored being their full autistic self at interview. We did a practice interview where I encouraged them to 'love their craft' which in this case was animals. As a result out poured all the years of expertise and insight they could bring to an employer. We discussed how an interview is two-way, and that if an employer rated you on eye contact or fidgeting, perhaps this is not an environment where you could work at your best, or be happy.

I am delighted to say that more employers are catching on to the value neurodivergent people bring. It feels like a ripple that is becoming a wave. Whilst stereotypes still abound, there are employers who are listening to autistic people (both outside of and within their workforce) and who are changing their interview processes so that autistic people experience better interviews and, therefore, are more likely to shine. Simple things such as having the questions printed, getting straight to technical questions and tightening up on vague questions where the meaning isn't clear. In all instances I see the company improves in general.

I notice a move away from a one-off initiative to recruit autistic people, and, from our community, an insistence that whenever you approach a company, no matter for what role, or whoever is sitting across the interview desk, that the company and its representatives should naturally accommodate you for who you are and the skills you bring, whether you are autistic or not, and that support should begin before diagnosis, and regardless of whether you disclose or not.

Work can be exciting, frustrating, exhilarating, fun, the place where you interact or not, or simply observe how others are or choose to be. Knowing how you work at your best and what makes you happy at work is a great starting point. I wish you well in your work journey.

Sharon Didrichsen
Founder and Director of Specialisterne NI

ACKNOWLEDGEMENTS

This book is dedicated to our feline friends Ernie Elley and Baz Campbell, because every author needs a muse – or in our case, mews.

Much as Ernie and Baz would like to claim full credit, we are indebted to Michael Barton, Sharon Didrichsen, Renata Jurkevythz, Cory Monteith, Daniel Rico and Shanan Slow for their invaluable feedback. Our thanks go to them for helping us ensure this book is useful, relevant and autistic-affirming.

We're in awe, quite frankly, of the talents of illustrator Tim Stringer who has brought our ideas to life with such wit. Thanks for being involved, Tim.

We're also very grateful to our patient commissioning editor and the whole team at Jessica Kingsley Publishers, who have taken on this unconventional guide and shown faith in its authors.

Finally, thanks to the readers who take the time to approach this book with an open mind and a hopeful heart. We hope you like it.

NOTES ON TEXT

We refer throughout the text to 'autistic people' rather than 'people with autism'. Most people we know prefer it that way, as they see autism as part of who they are – but it is entirely up to you how you choose to self-identify and we believe individual preferences should be respected. Having just finished writing this book, we both mostly identify as 'knackered'.

In this book we are generally literal with our wording, although we do use some idioms here and there. We haven't done this deliberately to befuddle you, honest. You'll notice that we've added the occasional explanation as a footnote if you need it. Our footnotes also explain any cultural references that you may not share with us, because we are decidedly ancient. Maura was, aptly, born to the strains of 'Please Release Me' by Engelbert Humperdinck whilst Debby emerged to Ray Stevens crooning 'Everything is Beautiful' (she does tend to look for positives).[1]

There's also an 'office idioms' guide in Chapter 20.

Since we're both based in the UK, if you live elsewhere some of our language may be different from what you're used to, but hopefully you'll still be able to work out what we mean. If it's any consolation, we only live 300 miles from each other but both use terms the other doesn't. Aren't words great?

---

1 Engelbert Humperdinck is a British pop singer and Ray Stevens is an American singer-songwriter and comedian. And thanks to them, we get to show you how the footnotes work.

PREFACE

Non-autistic adults (we hesitate to call them 'neurotypicals' because who *is* typical?) can be really odd when it comes to social settings.

It turns out, however, that in the workplace they can be even more confusing, with another set of unwritten social rules that apply purely to the office.

Of course – as per usual – none of these little rules are actually explained. People expect that they are just 'known' – granted from birth by a social skills fairy.

Who knew that having a desk next to someone meant that you were obliged to be a bit politer to them? *How very draining*, if they happen to be annoying.

Plus, when people experience the world differently, they may find it hard to understand each other when interacting.[1] However, whereas autistic people are only too aware that adapting to others' approaches is useful – they've generally had to do it all their lives – non-autistic people don't always meet you half-way by making an effort in return.

So, now that you've worked hard to get yourself a career, we'd hate to see it wasted just because the social skills fairy didn't tell

---

1   This is what Dr Damian Milton calls 'the double empathy problem' (2012). Different experiences impact on people's ability to empathize with each other and this is likely to be exacerbated, according to Milton, through differences in language use and comprehension.

you the office stuff, so here's a handbook to help you fathom out what the heck is going on and to decode the mysterious ways of the neuro-majority. In this book, we'll also guide you about how to enlighten your colleagues on autism as it affects you, if you want to, so they understand you better and will (hopefully) make more of an effort in return.

Who are we and why do we think we can we help? That's a fair question.

Autistic author and screenwriter Maura Campbell lives in Northern Ireland. Maura has been working in an office for over 30 years – not the same one – so has had plenty of time to study what goes on and figure out what's expected (kind of like David Attenborough in *Frozen Planet*,[2] but without the penguins). As well as writing, she has enjoyed a varied and interesting career in the civil service, mostly because civil servants are, well, civil.

Over the Irish Sea typing away at her own keyboard, Manchester-based Debby Elley has two autistic sons, one of whom is about to embark on the daunting world of work himself. Having written for autistic families for 15 years as the co-founder of *AuKids* magazine and as an author, her main interest is in helping autistic people to grow and adapt without changing who they really are. She's also passionate about helping people to support the autistic population by understanding them a bit better, and allowing them to play to their strengths.

Debby read Maura's books, and Maura read Debby's. We both decided that we had to work together, as we had very similar writing styles and the same rather irreverent humour...

We hope that this book, written by an autistic (Maura) and non-autistic (Debby) team, joined by an autistic illustrator, Tim

---

2   UK TV series about the natural world featuring – you guessed it – a lot of penguins.

Stringer, will help you to settle in more quickly to a job and be happier and more successful.

Don't be daunted. You don't have to change. There is nothing 'wrong' with you or how you think and you shouldn't have to adopt a fake persona just to make other people more comfortable. Instead, we're trying to help you understand other people's reactions in certain situations, so that you can decide for yourself how to respond. We know how anxiety-inducing it can be when things feel a bit 'off' but you're not sure why.

Just a smattering of these new insights and a bit of awareness about those non-autistic colleagues of yours should work wonders. Whether you then adjust your approach is completely up to you.

What we'll never ask you to do is to behave in a way that feels unnatural or inauthentic. First, that's a recipe for burnout if you keep it up for sustained periods of time, and second, asking people to bend themselves out of shape is hardly conducive to creating an inclusive workplace.

At the end of the day, our mission is to create a better understanding between you and your new work colleagues. How you respond to our suggestions is unique to you, and that's the beauty of this book. Take what works well for you.

Come back to this book if you can't absorb it all at once. Unlike people who give verbal advice, the big advantage of us writing this is that we're always here (even when you don't actually want us, a bit like a repeat of *Friends*[3]), so you can read us as slowly as you want to, and as many times as you want to.

There's only one *you* and the world needs your skills. We hope you find this guide useful – and best of luck sharing your talents and knowledge with the world!

---

3 Long-running popular American TV comedy series that's endlessly being repeated. And we mean ENDLESSLY.

CHAPTER 1

WHY BOTHER WITH AN OFFICE?

(It's a valid question)

If you enjoy working alone, you might wonder why anyone would bother putting themselves through the trouble of getting up early and going to an actual office building. Surely it would be better to stay at home in your pyjamas with the laptop perched on your duvet?

Well, yes, you're right. It might well be more comfortable.

If you're anything like us, you do your best work in quiet surroundings with few interruptions. Autistic people thrive in their comfort zones – environment is everything. So if you're most productive and happy in your own environment, then it's a practical and logical idea to think about working from home.

In fact, to the authors of this book, it's always been obvious that many people enjoy working from home and can do it quite effectively. Everyone needs time in their day to load the washing machine and make a fuss of the cat (or dog/guinea pig/budgie/lizard – delete as necessary).

Although this *was blatantly obvious*, companies have historically expected their employees to squeeze their home lives around office hours.

Lockdowns during the Covid pandemic forced organizations to think again. Bingo! Lots of people now work from home, at least some of the time if not all of it, quite successfully. This is a win-win; employees are happier with the flexibility, and companies now save lots of money on expensive offices full of drab furniture, unfathomable coffee machines and half-dead pot plants.

So as we write this book, you will be entering a job market that may well be far more relaxed about people working from home at least some of the time, particularly if you have chosen to work in technology. Of course, this won't work for everyone – it depends what career you want.

> **Joke alert:** Working from home if you're a midwife might not be much help to anyone.

Before we get carried away and wonder why anyone might bother to write a book about office life at all, you will still need to work with other people even if you're home based. Much of this book will provide you with guidance on how to deal with them profession-ally, especially when faced with challenges. We have also written a chapter especially for those whose jobs are 'hybrid' with working hours shared between the office and home (see Chapter 13).

Here are some other things about working in actual buildings to consider:

Advantages to an office

1. Working in an office can make communication quicker and better

Waiting for e-mail responses can slow things up, but if you're in the same office you can just walk to someone's desk when it's con-venient and ask them. When you talk to someone in person, they might give you suggestions or opinions that they wouldn't bother with in a hurried e-mail.

Also bear in mind the e-mail of the species is more deadly than the mail...

We can explain...

Because people receive so many e-mails in an average working day, they usually scan them quickly and fire off a reply so they can move onto something else. Sometimes they might misinterpret your e-mail or the tone you've used. When that happens, you can end up in a confusing and frustrating back-and-forth that ends up taking much longer than if you'd just talked in person.

Most office disputes have their origins in miscommunication. Things can escalate quickly when e-mail is involved and before you know what's happening it's turned into a right kerfuffle.

If you don't understand what is meant in an e-mail to you, it's worth talking to someone in person – or at least telephoning them. Here's where the office can come into its own.

2. Office spaces help you to swap ideas and learn

One of the main advantages of being in an office when you're new to a career is that you can learn a tremendous amount by being around more experienced employees. Most people are very generous with their wisdom.

Sometimes, there's nothing better than sitting in a room with others and talking about ideas. When people work well together, you can get a satisfying synergy – producing something that's well beyond what you could do on your own.

3. Offices can develop your social circle

Ha ha ha ha ha.

Yes, we know. Working *plus* being sociable might seem the most stressful combination you can think of, but some peculiar souls actually go to work in an office *because* of the contact with other people.

People who struggle to focus for hours can find it a bit of a relief to have little chats every now and then. A meeting here, a coffee there, a quick break whilst someone asks you whether you've seen that funny meme.

You may be the kind of person who likes to focus for a long time when you're absorbed in something. In fact, as you're autistic, we'll bet that you're more capable of focusing for long stretches of time than most of your colleagues.

You may well even find interruptions a bit aggravating.

It's worth considering, however, that if you're doing a job that you genuinely enjoy and it makes use of some of your particular skills, then one great way to meet like-minded people is to work with them. In workspaces people can sometimes make friends for life, even find life partners. (Best to get to know them first before you drop to one knee and propose, though. You don't want to discover too late they're a Justin Bieber[1] superfan if you're most definitely not one. We are talking from personal experience, here.)

If you're the sort of person who is used to being a bit isolated but you didn't really plan it that way, this could be something of an opportunity. We're not denying that it's a challenge, but you may benefit from it.

4. Being in an office can lead to opportunities

If you're quietly working away at your home computer, then you may not hear about opportunities within the company to advance your career. You might not get spotted as easily when it comes to a new project or a promotion opportunity. It's far easier when you are hearing and seeing what's going on in your working environment to stay connected to the office news.

---

1 Very successful Canadian singer. According to Wikipedia (2023) he's sold over 150 million records worldwide.

Is it for you?

The key to working this out is knowing yourself.

Consider how you've done your best work in the past, whether that's been on your own or with other people around you.

Think about whether you are great at getting work done at home, or whether like us you start to find the thought of tidying your sock drawer more inviting than actually doing any work, and you need a more formal environment to motivate you.

Maybe you need a structure to your day and find that tricky to impose on yourself. Or maybe generating your own daily structure suits you more.

Most of all, think about what it is you want to do. Perhaps you already have enough ideas and expertise to be your own boss. On the other hand, you might welcome being in an environment where you can pick up skills and experience from others.

That's a lot of things to consider. Being honest with yourself and your own needs is important, though, if you want to choose a pathway that gives you the best chance of being happy.

You may find it helpful to talk these things through with those who know you well. There is no perfect answer, as there are strengths and drawbacks to every kind of work.

Just reassure yourself that if you do step into an office, no one is bolting the door behind you and jangling the jail keys. If you really don't like it, you can just leave and try somewhere else.

Similarly, if you are at home and find that you are so isolated that the most meaningful conversation you've had all week was with Siri,[2] it might be time to change pathways and apply for a job in a team...

So – you've never worked in an office before. What's it like? Read on...

---

2   Apple Inc.'s digital voice assistant.

CHAPTER 2

WHAT IS AN OFFICE LIKE?

Offices are a bit like dogs. Let us explain.

Most are friendly and they are likely to have several features in common.

For example, they have four walls, a roof and nylon carpet with enough static electricity to power the photocopier. After that, they may come in a wide variety of shapes and sizes.

Office layouts

Open plan offices are pretty common these days. You may be told it's so that people can communicate better but it's usually because they're cheaper. 'Open plan' means there's a large room with lots of desks – kind of like a library but without as many books.

Sometimes there are partitions surrounding each desk, or particular areas, but these may not be enough to lock out the loud breathing or really annoying laugh of your co-worker in the next cubicle.

It's less common to have a room of your own these days, unless your job requires it, though you may share with a couple of people.

Meeting rooms

Some organizations have one or more separate rooms for small group meetings or for when you need a private chat. They're usually called a break-out room (not to be confused with an escape room, though you may well fantasize about legging it[1] if the meeting feels like it's lasting forever).

Our favourite, though, is the boardroom. Not because it might have wood panelling or a convincing fake potted plant to impress visitors. No, it just amuses us that the name of a room in which long meetings are held sounds like 'bored room'. Call us literal. Or maybe we should just get out more.

Your desk or mine?

Whilst every office is laid out differently, most have lots of desk space and people usually have a computer or laptop each. You might be given your own landline phone, or it could be a shared one.

If your company has 'hot desks', they aren't desks that make you go 'ouch!' Hot desking just means that you sit wherever there's a space. If the company works this way, you may need to put your stuff in a locker at the end of the day.

Office hours

Whether you're working in an office or from home, you'll be expected to work for a certain number of hours each week. Unlike school, nobody will ring a bell to let you know when to start, stop or take a break.

The full-time working day is usually eight hours a day with an hour's break for lunch. For quite a lot of people, that's 9am–5pm,

---

1   Dashing out.

but not always. If someone says they're at their desk 'during office hours' they do tend to mean between Monday and Friday, 9am–5pm.

Some companies can be flexible about the hours you work. If you're working in a tech company and communicating online with people in different time zones abroad, for instance, you might well work hours that allow you to be working when they're awake.

If you're working from home, there could be more flexibility about hours. The important thing is that you'll know before you start work how many hours you're expected to work each day.

Office dress code

Ooh, this can be a tricky one. What's deemed to be appropriate office attire can vary considerably between organizations. You might get away with Bermuda shorts and a Hawaiian shirt in a tech start-up but that mightn't go down so well in a law firm, for instance. Or front-of-house in a funeral parlour. You get the point.

Unless you have got this one sussed during a familiarization visit – we'll explain about that a bit later – it's probably best to show up wearing something reasonably smart for your first day. What do we mean by 'reasonably smart'? We're really just talking about a step up from jeans and a T-shirt here – so trousers or skirt with a shirt or blouse. A little bit smart, but not a suit, is what people sometimes refer to as 'smart casual' (Smart? Casual? Make your flipping mind up, why don't you?).

Once you're there, you can take a look at how other people are interpreting the dress code to help you decide what to do after that. You might find some folks are dressed smarter than others, which may be because they're more senior or because they have a meeting with clients. So take your cue from the people who have a similar role in the office to you.

If it calms you to wear something associated with an interest,

but you need to look smart, you could try sneaking it into your dress code, for instance, by wearing a Pokémon tie or socks. Or, wear a subtle badge to give you the comfort of your favourite hobby without having it blasted all over a T-shirt.

For some with touch sensitivities, dressing smartly is very difficult. Debby visited a hi-fi repair shop recently where everyone was dressed in uniform except for one individual whose expert knowledge and enthusiasm had no doubt caused his boss to relax the dress code.

So, depending on the environment and your manager, there may be flexibility. If you can't focus on your work without wearing something really comfortable, mention it after being offered the job and see what can be arranged.

TOP TIP: HIDDEN CHARMS

No one looks at underwear, so personalize that as much as you want! One of our friends has to wear blue, and has told us: 'If you can't see it on me, I'm wearing blue underwear!' A little too much information, here, but the point is it worked for him.

CHAPTER 3

THE ADAPTABLE OFFICE

Asking for reasonable adjustments... er, reasonably

I f they are aware you are autistic, employers have a duty by law to make what's referred to in legalese as 'reasonable adjustments'.[1]

This chapter gives a general overview of what types of adjustments you might be able to request as well as when and how to do that. And, since we don't know everything (please don't tell our spouses), we've also included some notes in the support section at the end of the book on where you might be able to get some additional help or further information.

What are 'reasonable adjustments'?

These are changes employers might make to help you overcome any difficulties you may be experiencing. The clue is in the word

---

1   Whether or not you personally identify as disabled, autism is covered under the banner of disability under equality legislation (the UK's Disability Discrimination Act 1995 – still in force for Northern Ireland – and, for Great Britain, the Equality Act 2010, which forms part of the law of England and Wales, and with the exception of section 190 and Part 15, part of the law of Scotland).

'reasonable'. The principle behind the law on reasonable adjust-ments is that your workplace should be flexible enough to make changes if these won't radically interfere with the organization's ability to function and won't cost them more than they can afford.

Although your manager's idea and yours may be slightly differ-ent when it comes to what's considered 'reasonable', they should at least make an effort to be flexible where possible.

What's possible may depend on the size of the organization or the nature of what it does, so is different for every workplace. And, especially within larger organizations, some roles may be more adaptable than others depending on the duties involved. For in-stance, we imagine that if you have a new career as an undertaker, not a single employer will be flexible enough for you to wear your favourite rainbow-coloured T-shirt to work, even if a suit feels itchy. In contrast, the local gaming store might not mind at all. Bit of an extreme example, and yes you probably wouldn't choose anywhere to work that had an itchy uniform as compulsory work attire, but you get the picture.

Making automatic adjustments does require knowledge and experience. Some places will confidently state they are happy to provide 'reasonable adjustments' (or 'accommodations' if you are reading this in the USA) but when you ask them what adjustments are available, they may sound less certain. That's because although most employers are aware of the phrase 'reasonable adjustments', individual managers may not have had to put it into practice. That's where you can help – more on that in a moment.

Some employers may think of 'reasonable adjustments' as fairly large changes, which could make them slightly defensive if they assume these may be costly. They may be surprised to discover that often the changes required are relatively modest and some of them cost nothing.

Or, they might be worried about how other members of the team may react if it appears as though you're getting preferential treatment. It's sometimes incorrectly assumed that equality means treating everyone exactly the same, as opposed to creating a 'level playing field' (giving everyone an equal chance to succeed).

If ever you need to explain why adjustments aren't preferential treatment, consider using this cinema analogy:

> **Equality:** Suppose you were to visit a cinema, and all the seats were on flat flooring. You've booked a seat at the back and you can't see the screen. This is very unfair, especially if a very tall person is sitting right in front of you.
>
> Cinemas and theatres have raked (sloped) seats so that those people at the back have an equal chance to see the screen. They don't have an unfair advantage – it's not as if they're being given extra popcorn and more cushions. It's just that they are no longer at a *disadvantage* because of where they are sitting.

When to ask

Before you've been offered a job, you may feel slightly anxious about the prospect of a new environment. However, asking for a load of adjustments to the workplace at first interview is a bit like telling a person that you don't want to go for fish and chips on a first date when they haven't asked you out yet.

Once you've been offered the job, your prospective employer will hopefully want to be flexible with you, because in return they'll get a highly motivated employee whose approach could well be enhanced by a different outlook.

You may not need to ask for any adjustments straight away, or until you're certain you'll need them. Many people like to settle in first and find it easier to know what's needed after a few weeks in their new environment. If something is immediately obvious to you as a 'no-goer', i.e. you won't be able to do your job unless it's sorted swiftly, mention it to your manager and if your organization has a Human Resources department, you may be able to have a chat with them, too.

In order to seek adjustments, though, you may need to make your manager or employer aware that you're autistic. Which brings us on to...

To share or not to share?

Tricky one this, and very individual.

Some people would rather not share the information they are autistic for fear of causing the employer to jump to misguided assumptions based on watching too many episodes of *The Big Bang Theory*.[2]

Other people choose not to share it simply because they see it as no one's business. Plus, you may not fancy becoming a tick-box exercise to prove that a place is inclusive ('Ooh, autistic, yes please, our disability numbers are rubbish...').

We get all that.

On the other hand (looks at other hand), if you think you may well need some adjustments at interview or in your work environment, sharing the information that you're autistic at a reasonably early stage may work to your advantage. And if your employer 'actively welcomes applications from people with disabilities' then we'd say go for it.

If you decide to tell your employer or manager you're autistic, but you'd rather they didn't tell others, do request that they ask you before sharing it with anyone.

Despite any drawbacks you may be mulling over, there's a big advantage to making it known you're autistic at an early stage. If you do need to ask for flexibility or adjustments later, it should

---

2   American TV sitcom starring the character Sheldon, largely regarded as autistic.

be no great surprise to anyone and, therefore, not as big a deal to broach the subject. Plus, it allows others to advocate on your behalf, too.

Which brings us to the next pint... (we were going to say 'point' but predictive text got there before us and we found its wording preferable).

Delight in the difference

It's a good idea to ensure your new boss fully understands the positives of having you as an autistic employee and how autism has played to your advantage. For example, when talking about experience in research, you could say (if it's true) that being autistic means you can focus clearly for long periods of time and enjoy sifting through detail on a topic that interests you.

You don't need to mention autism in every darn sentence, but by referring to advantages and not just challenges, you'll ensure your employer will start to get a more balanced understanding of you. They'll also feel more comfortable asking you about it, which is a good thing as not asking can lead to ignorance... and ignorance is the place where assumptions like to hide. Assumptions are sneaky like that.

By the way, don't feel as if you've got to represent your entire neuroclan, here. You're a person in your own right, not an Autism Roadshow. It's enough to talk about how autism affects *you*. If a colleague starts to hopelessly generalize, or assumes you must love *Thomas the Tank Engine*,[3] don't feel the need to deliver a lecture, just point out that what they are saying may be true of some people, but not you.

(No judgement if you do happen to love Thomas. We're quite

---

3 A popular kids' TV show. It's commonly assumed among the non-autistic population that all autistic people are interested in trains.

fond of the useful little engine ourselves, even if he does promote rampant capitalism, economic exploitation and social stratification. Toot, toot!)

Using this approach, new employers get to know the true balance of autism as it affects you, rather than focusing purely on adjustments.

Try before you buy?

In much the same way as you probably had 'tester' afternoons for new schools and colleges, you might be able to suggest a brief visit to get a feel for the office environment before you accept a job offer.

Whether this can be facilitated, though, will depend on the organization. A smaller company with a lower number of applicants might be happy to show you around, for instance, whereas it might just not be practicable for a larger organization. If it's a bulk recruitment exercise,[4] for example, the people interviewing you may not end up being your manager.

But if a familiarization visit is a possibility, one way to suggest it might be something like: 'Working environment is quite an important thing for me, because I'm quite sensitive to... (*fill in sensitivity*). So, is it okay if I ask you some quick questions about that and have a look around the office?'

What to look for in your new workspace

If a visit isn't practical, don't worry. You should still be able to get help with meeting your particular needs after you've taken up a job offer.

---

4   Recruiting large numbers of people, sometimes university graduates, at the same time.

The sorts of things you might want to look out for in your new office space will depend on your own sensory profile. Have a good look around your new surroundings and try to identify anything that may prove problematic for you from the start.

We're now going to give you some examples of sensory issues that you may experience which, believe it or not, don't usually occur in those who don't have any sensory processing differences. And because it doesn't happen to them, they won't have thought of asking you about them or helping you to avoid them at all. People can't change what they don't know is a problem, so don't be shy about pointing out if something affects you quite a lot. Plenty of people are blissfully unaware that there are massive differences in how people experience their environment.

For starters, check out the noise levels in the office. Would you be able to cope with the ambient volume? Would you be sitting near a photocopier or something else that emits constant noise? Not everyone can hear electricity the way most autistics can. And most people can filter out background noise or other sensory inputs, rather than having a brain that needs to process *everything*. Must be nice for them.

If you're particularly sensitive to artificial lighting, check whether your workspace would be under a bank of fluorescent lights (or 'Satan's sunshine', as Maura likes to call them) that might pixelate your vision or give you ocular migraines.

Or, if smells are a sensitivity, are bins, toilets or a kitchen near to your desk?

These kinds of difficulties can usually be solved just by your manager being flexible on where you sit.

Your new employer may not be completely used to people who find the environment critical to their wellbeing, and so explaining this to them, in a relaxed way, may help them to understand why they should offer you some control over it.

Especially if they've just caught you sniffing the bins.

TRY NOT TO MAKE YOUR TOUR LOOK
LIKE A HEALTH AND SAFETY ASSESSMENT

What adjustments might you need?

Whether or not people know you are autistic, you may not have to make an official request for small adjustments. It might just be a matter of letting your colleagues know about your preferred ways of working.

Like everyone else, you'll have your own way of doing things and it's just a case of mentioning them if they affect other people at all. No big deal, when it doesn't really cost anyone anything. For instance:

- If sudden interruptions like phone calls tend to throw you off course, you could point out to people (politely) right from the start that you prefer e-mail or text rather than phone calls if they want to get hold of you, where possible.

- If you focus better on video calls with your camera switched off, just let people know that's your way of doing things and it helps you to focus. That way they'll know that you are engaged and paying attention, not playing Sudoku.[5]

- If someone has given a presentation, you can ask for a copy of the slides if you want to revisit the information.

- You could ask permission to record an important part of a meeting or presentation so that you can listen again.

- Don't be inhibited from wearing ear defenders or noise cancelling headphones if you need them. Maura keeps a set in her office for the weekly fire alarm test. The first time

---

5   Sudoku is a logic-based number puzzle that you can play online as well as on paper. Debby finds it more taxing than actually doing any work.

someone sniggered, she pointed out they were her equivalent of a ramp for a wheelchair user or a white stick for a blind person, not a funky fashion accessory.

- A friend of ours used to hand Debby any long company memos[6] and say: 'Can you summarize what this is about?'

- You could ask for a larger font or text typed in blue rather than black, or on coloured paper.

- You could ask to remain at a desk where the lighting and noise levels are preferable.

There may be other kinds of adjustments you need that will involve making a more formal request, such as specific equipment and adaptations to the standard terms and conditions of employment. Here's a couple of examples:

- If overhead lights bother you, asking for an uplighter or desk lamp instead.

- Asking for an adjustment in your working hours to avoid crowds or to work around any medication you may be taking.

Asking for adjustments

If you know what you need, then giving the reason why you need an adjustment will help. For example, if you're feeling a sudden urge to throw the printer out of the window because it's smashing

---

6 Short for memorandum – an organization's written communication to its employees.

your concentration into a million little pieces, saying 'the printer's too loud', isn't quite reflecting what you're going through. 'I've got extremely sensitive hearing and so the printer sounds much louder to me than to other people – please could I move away from it?' is way preferable. Now they understand the real problem.

Plus, no windows (or printers) have been broken.

Try to avoid phrasing your needs in a negative way, since this could mean that your employer forms a picture of helplessness and difficulty. You really don't want unintentionally to give that impression, because it's not true.

How do you phrase it more positively, then?

Great question.

Below you'll see our trusty chart showing different ways of asking for the same thing. On the left-hand side, our language gives the impression of someone struggling, what we'll call 'Poor Cinderella' language.

On the right, using positive language to present things differently, we've played Fairy Godmother and magically given the impression of someone competent, able to thrive with just a few adjustments. We'll call that kind of positive phrasing 'Ball Cinderella' (cos it's the magical successful version).

People are more receptive when you focus on what *can* be done, rather than what *can't*.

This concept is one of our golden nuggets[7] in this book, so watch out for it again, it's one of our favourite topics!

'Poor' Cinderella is struggling...	'Ball' Cinderella is winning...
I *can't* work if there's too much noise...	I'm a bit sensitive to a lot of noise, so I focus *far better* if I'm in a quiet space in the office.

cont.

---

7   Best pieces of advice.

'Poor' Cinderella is struggling...	'Ball' Cinderella is winning...
I find it *hard* to focus if it's warm in the office.	I can be quite sensitive to temperature, so I'd like to bring in a fan for my desk. It *helps* me to work *better* if it gets a bit warm.
It *really gets to me* when there's lots of noisy machinery about.	I can see you've got quite a few machines here, because of noise sensitivity I find I work *much faster* if I'm not too close to them, is that okay?

So, to recap: you want your employer to think: 'Hey, potentially we have a really keen, productive employee here who just needs a few adjustments!' rather than 'Oh wow, if they are moaning about everything NOW, what the blooming heck are they going to be like in a month's time?'

In short, if you have ways of working that make life easier, and they don't particularly inconvenience anyone else, be quite straightforward with those requests.

If you need a larger change than that, ask your boss for an adjustment and let them know why it's important to you.

Getting outside help with adjustments

If your employer is being resistant, or you can't say what you need because you don't actually know, you may need to seek some outside assistance.

Whilst the support you can access will depend on where you are geographically speaking, there should be help available. At the end of this book, you'll find some extra advice about where to go for support in getting changes made to your workplace.

CHAPTER 4

OFFICE SMALL TALK

N on-autistic people love talking crap. What's more, they're really excellent at it.

Why do they insist on talking about the weather, something only they watched on TV, or other things that are of little interest?

Well, in psychological terms, we call these 'social strokes'.

It turns out that for most of your non-autistic colleagues, small daily greetings, combined with a bit of small talk, can have a surprisingly positive impact on their wellbeing.

Yeh, that's right. It's that weird.

A 'social stroke' is not a medical condition, but a term for the positive feelings that we give to someone simply by saying 'Hi' and acknowledging they exist. It's a metaphorical version of stroking our pets, except for this is a quick 'Hello, how are you doing?' rather than tickling someone under the chin like you might do with a fluffy pal, which we suspect wouldn't go down very well with the Human Resources department.

If you're autistic, the trouble with being asked how you are is sometimes the *answering* bit. It's a very open question with no obvious right answer. Worrying about what you should say in return can create anxiety. So, to autistic people, small talk doesn't always feel so much like a 'social stroke' as a clobber around the back of the head with a rubber hammer.

Small talk can be defined as having a conversation about something inconsequential, rather than anything deep and meaningful, that doesn't relate to work.

If you don't like small talk, you don't like it. Don't worry, you don't have to force it. People are quickly aware of those who like a bit of small talk and those who don't. You won't be alone by the way; plenty of non-autistics hate it too.

What we'd like to share, if you'll allow us to, is what some non-autistics tend to expect when they use it. What you do with that information is very much up to you, but we wouldn't want you to be caught out by simple misunderstandings.

Tip 1: When people greet you, they expect a simple answer
If you're being greeted with 'How are you?' or 'Everything okay?' then usually no one genuinely wants to know. That's just the non-autistic way of saying 'Hi'. What they really should be saying to avoid confusion is:

'How are you? – in ten words or fewer and keep it upbeat'.

The expected response is 'Fine' or 'Yes, thanks – and you?' rather than an exposition on the myriad geopolitical, economic and sociological reasons we should be collectively embraced by existential angst.

Yeh, so probably best not to go into too much detail.

Tip 2: Non-autistics make massive assumptions
Non-autistics expend quite a lot of energy trying to appear pleased to see people they'd rather ignore. This is because it makes the working atmosphere easier. When faced with blunt honesty, they don't cope very well.

When someone greets you, if you don't greet them in return, the more delicately minded of your office colleagues might panic and assume they've done something to upset you.

A quick acknowledgement of the type that suits you is all that's required. You might want to raise your hand in a little wave without looking up from your computer if you're not particularly fussed about starting a conversation. Some people have perfected the art of smiling at someone's forehead if they don't want eye contact. Acknowledging people can make them feel accepted, which leads to an easy-going working environment.

Tip 3: When others expect a little more

If the art of conversation gives you the shivers and someone has actually stopped to talk to you rather than just passing by and saying 'Hi', you could just ask them how they are and what they are up to at the moment. Or maybe ask them how work's going. Many non-autistics will eagerly embrace the opportunity to talk about themselves. Job done! If you don't want to chat at all, you can easily get rid of them with a friendly 'Hi – bit busy at the moment...' and they'll hopefully get the hint and move away.

Tip 4: It's a chat, not a test

Autistic people sometimes get really concerned about conversations because they can't process auditory information fast enough.

TOP TIP: RELAX

When you're making small talk, do remember that most non-autistics won't remember everything that you say. Or in some cases, they won't remember any of it. You shouldn't, therefore, put enormous pressure on yourself to remember their own news and views.

Your average office worker views social bonding as more important than being able to recall any actual conversation.

So, think of small talk as purely a bonding experience and not an exchange of important information – then you won't place as many demands on yourself.

You could be forgiven for thinking that small talk is a complete waste of time. It's true that small talk doesn't get things done, but it can help build good relationships and give you a rough idea of how people are likely to respond when you're working together. It sets a good foundation for working with that person that will make it much easier to tackle any difficult work issues together in the future.

Tip 5: Stick to safe topics
Office chat in small groups tends to centre around popular culture and sport because lots of people know about these things, and you don't have to get too in-depth.

Talking about the weather is a good one, because non-autistic people have an insatiable interest in meteorological conditions (*and they think we're the obsessive ones? – Maura*).

Early in the week, you can always ask somebody if they had a good weekend – and later in the week you can ask them if they have plans for the weekend ahead.

Don't ask us what you should do on a Wednesday.

Once again, think 'bonding' rather than 'information exchange'. So, for instance, if *they* ask *you* about your weekend plans, don't feel you ought to provide a detailed itinerary. The edited highlights are fine, like saying you're going to the cinema or for a nice walk. Also, don't feel that the question means you're *compelled* to have an action-packed weekend planned – you can just say you're looking forward to relaxing at home.

Tip 6: Avoid giving too much information

Getting over-familiar a bit too soon is something we'll come to in Chapter 8. Too much personal information can have the bewildering effect of scaring people off, when you were just being friendly!

Think of it this way: imagine that the information you hold about yourself is like a box of gems. Some of them are truly valuable and rare, others are just semi-precious stones and others pretty glass. Would you give your most valuable gems away to anyone? Of course not, you'd save them for those closest to you or maybe only for yourself.

If you scatter your own diamond collection – very personal information – to people you don't know that well, you give it less value. People are used to keeping their own personal information to themselves, and so it feels wrong to them if you're too free and easy with things that are personal to you.

The best advice we can give is to start with the basics, focusing on talking about previous work or education experiences, and work up gradually to telling people more about your home life as they share more with you.

So what are your 'diamonds', then? How about...

- Your private life, including arguments between you and family members or between you and your partner if you have one. You can mention if you have a partner, and what they do for a living, but leave out more personal information regarding stresses in the relationship or physical intimacy.

- A personal grievance with someone, and why you'd like to own a dartboard with their image on it. Save that for the people closest to you.

- Ailments, unless they keep you off work, and even then you only have to tell the boss and you don't have to go into too much detail. For example, 'An operation on my toe' is better than talking about the moment you realized that your toe didn't look right, the constant pain in your foot, the way it looks up close, etc.

• Anything to do with your personal hygiene ('I didn't have clean underwear today so I put on yesterday's instead').

TOP TIP: PRIVATE MATTERS

You can of course mention if you are concerned about a family member who is ill; although this is personal, if you're worried about someone and it may impact your work, it can help others to know why you may not be that cheerful at the moment.

Equally, it is your absolute right not to mention if someone else's illness is worrying you. However, it's always a good idea to confide in your boss if you feel your work may be affected by something that is going on at home.

If you personally have an illness that's worrying you, it's best to keep it to those you really trust at work – and your boss.

It pays to know that religion and politics can generate strong feelings and in-depth chats rather than small talk. Plus, once people start talking about politics, it can be kind of hard to stop them.

Also, avoid being conscripted into the 'culture wars' – hot topic social issues that divide people into warring factions. Be aware that just because somebody seems nice, it doesn't mean they necessarily share your views.

If a quick friendly chat about the weekend or TV the night before is all that's expected, then your non-autistic colleagues may swerve (avoid) you if they feel every greeting will end up in the equivalent of a televised debate. Be aware that if people do not share the same passions, it takes them a lot of energy to listen to your views, especially if they have work on their mind.

If you do feel highly passionate about a topic, you could say 'I've got rather strong views on that one'. That will give people the warning they need and then they can decide whether to start a lengthy chat or not.

Tip 7: Check whether someone shares your favourite topic
Hey, if you want to talk about your favourite topic and share it with others, that's awesome. How can you tell if they aren't that interested, though?

In conversation, people can listen to someone for about a minute without joining in at all. If this isn't a subject that really interests them, and they can't join in the chat, after about a minute they may begin to run out of what we call 'listening patience'.

One clue that someone's lost interest is their answers to what you say will become shorter, possibly just single words like 'yep'. If they are sitting opposite you, their body will tell you before their face does! They may start shuffling papers or looking back down at their monitor; this shows they are getting impatient to move onto their work. When they are standing, their feet may start pointing away from you, showing they intend to leave. They may physically take a shuffle away from you. When sitting, they may swing their chair back around to their computer so only their head is pointing in your direction. If someone is really attentive, their entire body points towards you, and they'll possibly lean forward, too.

One great way to avoid getting carried away in your own thing is to use a 'trial question'.

A conversation without a trial question might go like this:

Alison asks Robert what he did at the weekend.
'I went to a gaming convention', Robert says.
'Oh really? That sounds good', replies Alison.

She is showing an interest, so Robert talks about every celebrity YouTuber at the convention until Alison is just nodding but not saying anything at all.

This is fine for Robert, as he is having a really great conversation with himself and quite enjoying it. Alison, however, ran out of listening patience after about a minute because she couldn't join in.

Here's how the trial question works:

'I went to a gaming convention', Robert says.

'Oh really? That sounds good', replies Alison.

'Yeh it was great. Are you into gaming?' asks Robert.

There's the trial question, which has assessed how interested Alison is, or whether she's just being polite. When Alison says that it's 'not really her thing' but she liked The Legend of Zelda,[1] Robert can keep his explanations a bit shorter and focus on chatting about Zelda instead.

This may feel deeply unfair to Robert, since talking about the convention makes him happy, but at least he's now aware enough to know how to pitch his conversation without losing Alison's interest. Unfortunately, the average non-autistic person probably doesn't want to be given the equivalent of a lecture.

TOP TIP: TRIAL QUESTIONS

Test out someone's interest before starting a long talk about something. If only non-autistics used the trial question: 'Are you into small talk?'

---

1   The Legend of Zelda is an action-adventure game franchise from Nintendo.

Autistic folks can find it easy to info-dump, simply because it's more comfortable talking about a favourite topic than listening and processing.

But it's not all one-sided. Non-autistic people tend to do this too, only they tend to focus on wittering about other people, rather than things. So, you might find yourself glazing over when Alison decides to talk to you about her cousin's neighbour's son's autism (which you're bound to be interested in, of course, you being autistic too and everything... and yep, we're being sarcastic).

Apparently, boring others with chat about people they're never likely to meet is more socially acceptable than boring people with details of a hobby that they don't share.

No, we don't get it either.

CHAPTER 5

OFFICE LANGUAGE

Acronyms, jargon and slang, oh my!

When you first start working in an office, you may quickly feel as if you've arrived in a foreign land. These people have their own language!

It happens in every office. Groups of people develop their own shorthand for common business terms and it becomes so familiar to them that they barely even notice they're doing it.

Three letter abbreviations (or TLAs... hee hee hee)

For instance, in Maura's office world, they had abbreviations such as MIR (management information report) and acronyms such as CaMaS (case management system). These were used fairly regularly and so they became part of Maura's office 'language'.

By the way, in previous books we have had to remind professionals that when it comes to autism not everyone understands ADOS, ASD, ASC, SLT, OT, SPD and so on.[1] The autism arena is

---

1 Autism diagnostic observation schedule; autism spectrum disorder; autism spectrum condition, speech and language therapist, occupational therapy, sensory processing disorder. (We're not saying you're disordered, just giving some examples of terminology professionals tend to use.)

incredibly rich with befuddling jargon, and people sometimes use it to look clever when they don't quite understand what they're talking about, which really annoys us.

Common office initialisms

There are some more common initialisms (abbreviations in the form of initials) used in the office world in general, so here's a handy guide to the ones we know best. They're generally used in e-mails or texts rather than spoken, you'll be relieved to hear. We hope they are, at least, otherwise the person who wants to tell you they're out of office ('O-O-O') may well get confused for Santa.

Don't bother learning them, or worrying about them. They're here so that you're aware they exist. We had to look up some of them, as not every office is full of initialism junkies.

Why do people use these? One word: laziness. More charitably, it could be that they have large fingers and typing long messages is troublesome.

But more likely, laziness.

COB: Close of business

EOD: End of day – same as close of business

EOW: End of week

ETA: Estimated time of arrival

FTE: Full-time employee (or full-time equivalent)

FYI: For your information

HR: Human Resources

IAM: In a meeting

LET: Leaving early today

OOO: Out of office

OTP: On the phone

NRN: No reply necessary

PTE: Part-time employee (or part-time equivalent)

SME: Subject matter expert
TLDR: Too long, didn't read (anyone who likes abbreviations this much will undoubtedly have a short attention span)
WFH: Working from home
YTD: Year to date

The jargon monster

When Debby worked for a newspaper back at the turn of the century (21st, not 20th, cheeky), there was all sorts of journalism jargon. There were by-lines, vox pops, subs, proofs and spreads... But the best one was when she was told she had left an orphan at the bottom of a page. A kindly soul explained that 'orphan' was the term for the first line of a paragraph 'abandoned' at the bottom of a newspaper page all by itself.

If someone uses an abbreviation or jargon that you don't understand, that isn't down to you being ignorant, that's just down to you being new. Don't feel worried or out of your depth. We've all been there.

> ### TOP TIP: ASK EARLY
> Never, we repeat never, feel awkward asking for clarification. Leaving it too late, and pretending to understand, may cause you difficulties later. Ask early and make a note.

Have the confidence to say 'Apologies, I haven't come across that before – what does that stand for?' No one should think any less of you. It's always better to ask for an explanation than nod and pretend you understand, as it's far easier asking questions in the early days than later on when people assume that you know.

It's also a good idea to make a note of new terminology specific to your workplace so that you can refresh your memory and not ask repeatedly.

Office terms for performance

Your 'performance', you'll probably have gathered, is a word for how you're doing at work. PRP stands for 'performance related pay', as in certain workplaces (not all, by any means) your pay is calculated according to your performance. If your office uses PRP, it will be openly stated in the terms of your employment and may be mentioned at your interview.

Quarters

In industries where profits are important, companies talk about 'quarters' when they mean quarter of a financial year. The financial year, when annual accounts are done, starts on April 1st. So, the first quarter of a year is the three months from April to June. Managers tend to look at how their company is doing every 'quarter' and analyse patterns to see how the year is shaping up.

Appraisals

Your annual review (like a school report, but with a meeting to discuss progress and more opportunities for you to talk back!) is sometimes called an appraisal or performance review. More about them later in Chapter 15.

Idioms and phrases

Traditionally, office workers are idiom speakers without any respect for either anyone who speaks English as a foreign language or, for that matter, the literal mind. Sorry about that. By now we suspect that you know plenty of idioms, enough to be aware of when one is being used, at least, which is great. However, you may not have come across some of the phrases particularly used in the world of work, so here's where we are concentrating our efforts now.

Warning: the grown-up world of idioms at work doesn't mean that they're any more meaningful than the ones you recognize from your school days.

Cricket metaphors are especially popular – 'close of play' (end of the day), 'on the back foot' (starting at a disadvantage), 'knocked for six' (taken aback) and 'sticky wicket' (tricky situation), for instance.

If an idiom isn't of real importance to the conversation, some autistic people just get the general gist of what's being said and let it go, even if they're not that comfortable with the phrases used.

Management-speak tends to spread like a virus. You'll find that if a respected manager uses an idiom often, it spreads to their staff. New variants pop up all the time, usually after somebody's been off to a conference and been infected by a motivational speaker.

We can't really cover all of those confusing phrases. In fact, we had to cut back on them a bit otherwise we thought you'd fall asleep. Hopefully, though, this will give you some awareness of common ones.

If something sounds strange, you might consider whether literal thinking might be getting in the way of the meaning. For instance, 'running an eye over something' doesn't mean you're going to roll your eye like a marble across a spreadsheet.

Although, Maura does remember someone once asking their colleague to 'run an eye' over a draft before remembering they had a glass eye.

Awkward.

Our handy guide may be useful to a point, but it pays to be honest. If someone suddenly uses a phrase that affects your grasp of a topic, it's fine to ask for a translation from your fellow idiom speakers. You could say: 'That's not one I've come across before...' or just joke, 'Nope, the literal mind cannot translate that one!'

There's no shame in misunderstanding idioms, and those around you will learn to adapt and avoid them, or explain them, if you're honest about them getting in the way of your understanding.

Managers educated at posh schools may also litter their prose with references to ancient Greek mythology in the hope of inspiring their staff. All they usually get in reply is 'Eh?'

I guess what we're saying is that it's okay if you don't understand all of someone's poetic references. If you get the general gist, that's okay. You don't have to read up on the classics.

Here are some of our favourite office idioms and phrases. They are all repeated, and loads more added, in Chapter 20, which we've dedicated as a handy guide to all kinds of befuddling comments.

Please bear in mind that since we are UK-based, these phrases may be more commonly used in that locality, and all countries have their own.

I need to get you up to speed...

I need to bring you up-to-date or teach you. For example, 'I'll get you up to speed on this new system'.

I'd like to reach out to you...

Urghh. We hate this one. 'Reach out' just means someone would like to communicate with you, but doesn't specify how. They aren't defining whether it would be by post, phone, e-mail, or face-to-face. Usually it's in an opening e-mail from someone you haven't met before, and you choose the method of contact. Or, choose to ignore them entirely if they're just trying to sell you something...

I just want to give you a heads up...

I'd like to give you advance warning. Thus, your head could do with being up to receive this information, rather than your head not really listening much and being bowed over whatever's more interesting, like TikTok.[2]

A busman's holiday

Means you are giving advice or doing work in your leisure time which is the same as the work you do for a living. For example, 'Bit of a busman's holiday for you, isn't it?' in which case avoid replying with 'I cannot drive a bus'. Or, do that for a joke and watch how everyone gets nervous about whether the literal thinker minds them laughing.

I'm clocking off or knocking off

Old factory term, means I'm going home now.

By the way, knocking off should generally be avoided these days, as in the UK it also means 'having sex with...' as in 'I heard he's knocking off his assistant...'

This does not mean that he and his assistant are both going home early. Although they probably will be.

Close of play

Sporting term for the end of the working day. If someone wants it 'on my desk by close of play' it means they want to see something by the end of the day.

My bad

This means 'that's my misunderstanding, sorry' (or 'my fault'). Terrible, isn't it?

Low-hanging fruit

The most easily achieved bit of a task. So, the task is being compared

---

2   TikTok is a popular platform for sharing very short mobile phone videos.

with a fruit tree where some of the lower fruit are easier to pick. For example, 'Well, let's not waste too much time and go for the low-hanging fruit first'.

Beautiful crap

We weren't sure whether our publisher would let us get away with the above sub-heading but we figured we made it this far, so why not try it...

'Beautiful crap' is our preferred term for empty phrases that are devoid of any real meaning but give the illusion of something profound being said.

Unlike jargon, abbreviations and idioms, which are confusing but actually mean something, 'beautiful crap' is often used to inspire or motivate people. When people brag about their company's aims to the public, their beautiful crap can make you doubt whether they are still speaking English.

If someone says a lot of words but you can't decipher much meaning, it's possible that there isn't actually much meaning to decipher. Usually, the thing they say first is the actual point, followed by a lot of what we call 'verbal wrapping paper' – they're just trying to make their first sentence sound important by using lots more words, or beautiful crap.

Or, what they're saying is so vague it's utterly meaningless – for example, 'It is what it is' or 'We are where we are'.

Although our examples of beautiful crap below are, like our idioms, generally recognizable to those who live in the UK, we are pretty darn sure that each country has its very own version of beautiful crap, and some even do it better than we do over here.

Here's a few examples of our favourite beautiful crap phrases.

'Let's take a holistic approach to this'.
Beautiful crap for taking everything into account.

'Let's be solution focused'.

Beautiful crap for let's solve the problem.

'We'll give it 110%'.

Beautiful crap for we'll give it our full attention (100%).

'Let's keep one step ahead of the curve on this!'

Beautiful crap for wanting to be the first to do things.

'Let's hit the ground running!'

This means getting going on something really quickly, rather than starting slowly. (So nothing to do with Wile E. Coyote.[3])

'We're against the clock on this one'.

Beautiful crap for 'Everyone hurry up'.

'We need to keep in the fast lane'.

Beautiful crap for 'Everyone hurry up'.

'Let's shift up a gear'.

Beautiful crap for 'Everyone hurry up'. Again.

'Let's pick up the slack'.

Yaaawwwwn. Beautiful crap for 'Everyone hurry up'.

Poetic phrases also constitute beautiful crap. 'We've safely brought this ship to shore' means 'Well done, everyone, the project is complete'. Anyone who starts talking about boats, mountains, rivers, rocky paths, etc. is probably talking beautiful crap to make what

---

3   Slapstick 1940s Looney Tunes / Merrie Melodies cartoon character who often ended up thwarted in his imaginative efforts to catch the Road Runner (a bird), falling off cliffs as a result.

they're saying sound a little more inspiring. In the UK, as the Covid lockdown eased, the then Prime Minister Boris Johnson (2021) started his speech with: 'The crocus of hope is poking through the frost'. Which was kinda nice, but still beautiful crap.

Best not to tell people when they're talking in beautiful crap. We'll keep that as our secret.

And don't feel too smug about the jargon usage – before you know it, you'll be doing it too.

It's as infectious as norovirus.

CHAPTER 6

FOOD AND DRINK

Autistic people often have the ability to get immersed in a task and a reluctance to emerge from that state until they're completely finished. Meanwhile, plenty of non-autistic workers prefer short periods of concentration punctuated by a tea break or a chat.

The office tea break is a great time for stretching your legs and having a little chat with colleagues. Non-autistics don't seem to be able to concentrate for very long without boiling a kettle – call it a ritual.

You may not drink either tea or coffee. However, it's a good skill to learn how to make them, as in smaller offices, people tend to take turns in making a drink for their colleagues. It makes you a good host at home, too! If you struggle because you don't personally have a caffeine addiction and, therefore, don't tend to make hot drinks, you can perhaps show willing by offering to help someone else out when they make the office drinks.

If you think you're probably going to break a mug because you're not very co-ordinated, get someone else to carry the tea tray. That way, if anything happens, they get the blame and not you. Ha ha.

We're all heart.

By the way, this applies to you whether or not you're autistic. Debby isn't a co-ordinated person and, having learnt the hard way, she ensures that she's never the one to carry the tea tray. She always explains to people that if they want their mugs in one piece, it's better that someone else does the carrying.

The drinks kitty

Not every office has a 'kitty', but just in case they do, here's what one is. In office-speak, 'the kitty' isn't actually a fluffy thing with pointy ears (sorry) but a joint fund. Often, this is used for buying tea, coffee and biscuits. We used to have jars that people would pop some money into at the beginning of the week. These days, with contactless payments so popular, it's more likely that you will take turns to buy some extras for the office. Unless the boss does it for you – in which case, way-hay!

If there are vending machines rather than a kitchen, you don't need to think about this.

Office mugs

Never use anyone else's personal mug. They will hunt you down. They will find you. They will ask why you used their mug. You will say, 'Because I didn't know it was yours'.

And Pam (for example) will say, huffily, something like: 'Well it's got *West Ham*[1] all over it'.

You will say, 'So?' and Pam will say, 'Well I'm a massive West Ham fan, aren't I?'

You will say, 'I did not know that'.

And Pam will say, 'Well you do now'.

Go for a boring mug (company logo, nothing of a personal

---

1   Football team from London, UK.

nature), or ask if it's anyone else's before using it. Or bring your own. Then you can also tell anyone off if they use it and be part of the Possessive About Mugs brigade.

(That's why we called her Pam.)

Sarcasm warning: Funnily enough, although you can't actually use anyone else's mug for a drink, you'll find you are more than welcome to wash it up and put it back in the cupboard for them.

If you do break someone's mug or chip it, turn the mug around in the cupboard so that it can't immediately be seen and don't admit to it. Feign shock and surprise when it's found, says Debby.

Oh okay, Maura told Debby she can't write that.

Own up to the breakage, then. Offer to buy them a new mug.

If they say, 'It's okay, you don't need to buy me a new one', they probably mean 'Yes, I darn well think you should, you crockery terrorist'.

So, we suggest you buy them a new mug. It will show thoughtfulness, even if they said they didn't want another. You may not be able to find the same design as the old mug (RIP), but if you find something similar it should genuinely be appreciated. If you can't find something similar without designing your own, don't worry too much about it, just a replacement mug will do nicely.

Sharing snacks

So, you've got some nice snacks on your desk. What should you share, and what should you keep as all yours?

If you have a large packet of biscuits or sweets, it's polite to offer your colleagues one. Not so that you'll be liked, just because it's a nice thing to do if you have plenty to go round and others will tend to do the same when they bring in snacks. We're not talking a treasured stick of KitKat™ here or offering your small bag of crisps around (they only put about ten crisps in packets these days anyway, have you noticed?). This is just if you have plenty of something.

You don't have to walk around like a waiter stopping at every desk, though. The main thing here is not to sit on your own chomping your way through oodles of cookies. Just ask the office in general if anyone would like one.

If chewing helps you to self-regulate, chewing gum is probably a slightly less intrusive way of satisfying that need than eating in front of others, not to mention it saves you from cleaning your keyboard from crumbs. Yeh, we think of everything.

Offered a bun? Just take one!

Literal thinking combined with a healthy appetite can get you into a bit of bother. For instance, non-autistics have a habit of saying 'Help yourself!' without actually specifying how many of something.

One poor chap was scolded by his colleagues when a staff member brought in her home-baked cupcakes and said to everyone 'Help yourself!' Taking her literally and first up to the table, he took three at once. Everyone else thought he was being rude. What was the problem?

The problem here is that office etiquette dictates you should make sure everyone gets a chance to take something before you hoard your own personal stash of goodies.

In another company, a fruit bowl in the reception area had a sign attached: 'Help yourself'. One staff member did exactly that and took the fruit bowl to his desk.

Usually, when someone says 'help yourself', they mean to take just one of something. By all means, if you're offered a second one, go ahead. Make sure to compliment someone on their home cooking if it's good, too, as it was thoughtful of them. Plus it will encourage them to keep doing more!

Meeting buffets

Sandwich buffets rely on a little self-control as you'll no doubt have your beady eye on your favourite fillings. It's okay to take three or four sandwiches at once, since they are generally not much bigger than postage stamps. Remember, though, to look at what's left for others first and be mindful that it all needs to be shared among the number of people in the room.

We usually find asking something like: 'Anyone mind if I take the last tuna one?' means that no one does mind, because you've been thoughtful enough to ask.

Shared fridges

If people bring their own food into the office, then there's sometimes an office fridge. An office fridge isn't like yours at home. Unfortunately, you can't just open it and pick up what you fancy. Treat anything in the fridge like someone's personal belongings unless it's collectively owned by the team. No touching anyone else's fancy yogurts. We know – we're total spoilsports.

And remember to clear out anything you put in there that's gone off. Nobody wants to have to own up to being the person who left a carton of milk in there so long it turned to cheese.

CHAPTER 7

BEING PART OF AN OFFICE TEAM

There is no 'I' in 'team'. There is also no 'we', but nobody (apart from us) seems bothered about that. This chapter gives you a few examples of how your non-autistic colleagues work as a team. (No gym kit required. Phew.) Here, we've pointed out a few easy ways that you can be tripped up when you don't know about office etiquette and how to avoid some minor pitfaaaaaallllllllllllllllllllllls (ooh, we just fell down a pitfall).

Equipment: Darn, it's not yours

If you're sharing an office with others, the chances are that you will also be sharing office equipment.

You'll probably hear a lot of requests for things that happen to be on your desk, like 'Can I just grab a pen from you?', 'Chuck me the stapler!' or 'Can I nick a Post-It?'

Throwing staplers is inadvisable if you're not very co-ordinated, by the way. They are very heavy and have a habit of landing on people's heads. For this same reason, don't try and be cool and ask someone to throw you the stapler if you know that you're no cricket captain. Getting a black eye from office equipment doesn't look very professional.

We're sorry to tell you that however fond of the blue stapler you are, and even if it's the only one that doesn't jam, unfortunately it isn't your pet stapler. People will take it from you and the cheeky so-and-sos will leave it at their own desks, too.

But that's okay, you can always take it back when you need it.

Getting possessive over office equipment is a sure way of annoying people, so try not to become Guardian of the Sellotape Dispenser.

This doesn't mean that others can steal your favourite pen if it belongs to you personally, so just keep that safe and don't leave it out on your desk. Good-looking pens are the first to be 'borrowed' and when we say 'borrowed' we mean that people have a great habit of forgetting to give them back.

Try to be good-humoured about anyone borrowing your pen and if you want it back, you could always ask for it in a light-hearted tone. Something like: 'Oi! Have you nabbed my favourite pen?!' or 'Ahem, I think you'll find that is my very special pen you seem to have acquired by mistake' should do the trick. If you're too serious over this stuff you could get labelled as petty.

Now with all that said, people do tend to refer to anything that usually lives on their desk as 'my...'.

So, if someone says: 'Who's nicked my stapler?' they just mean the one that *usually* lives on their desk.

Stop the hovver and end the bovver!

Just before you get the red pen out, this heading isn't a typo; we aren't talking about the office vacuum cleaner.

Hovering is when you walk up to someone's desk when they are in the middle of doing something else, and you stand there waiting for them to look up.

We know that it's very difficult to hold onto a thought or a question if you need an answer straight away and so you may well be tempted to 'hover' until someone pays attention to you.

It's good to be aware that if you have hovered for more than a few seconds and this person is still immersed in what they are doing, they are showing they don't want an interruption.

To the person hovering, it doesn't feel like you are interrupting, because you aren't saying anything. However, your hovering target can see you out of their peripheral vision and might find this off-putting, as your presence is a sign that you want them to rush what they are doing.

Being non-autistic, they are unlikely to be direct and say 'Go away', but this doesn't mean they're okay with it.

So, what can you do?

If the person you need is on the phone, you can always leave a note on their desk saying something like 'Could do with a chat when you're done'.

If the person you need is not on the phone, just ask: 'Have you got a moment?'

By introducing the idea that you need a minute or two of their time, you give them the option to tell you whether it's convenient, and if not now, when.

Giving timescales

We know that you probably prefer to be told in advance how long something's going to take.

Your awareness of this means that you have an advantage. Giving a rough timescale to others is a fantastic office skill.

So, when you do ask for help, let people know how much time you think you'll need.

'Hiya – I'm going to need about half an hour to go through this with you at some point... is that okay?'

'Hi. Could I have five minutes with you to discuss the project?'

"ANYBODY GOT A PAPERWEIGHT I COULD BORROW?"

You don't have to be accurate – no one knows how long a chat will take. But giving a rough estimate will help people to free up the right amount of time for you and know what to expect.

Asking for help in the right way means that people are far more likely to give you their time and energy. Huzzah!

A case of space

Sometimes, what someone else is doing looks way more interesting than your own work. It's worth noting, though, that as well as hovering by standing near someone's desk, hovering near their computer screen could feel a little intrusive to them.

A person's desk is their little home for the day, their mini fortress in a place where they haven't got much to call their own. So it's best to keep arm's length away when you're talking to them, and avoid getting too close to their screen unless they've invited you to look at it.

And yes, this still applies even if they're attempting Wordle[1] on their lunchbreak and you've already solved it.

Mood monitoring

One of the things that's hardest work in an office (for everyone, not just autistic people) is trying to work out what mood others are in.

This is important, as you don't really want to be asking the boss for a favour if they've just had an argument with their spouse.

Similarly, if a client has just got on your colleague's nerves, this might not be the time to break the bad news to that colleague about an upcoming deadline.

Before you make a demand on someone, think about the mood

---

1   A web-based word game created by Welsh software engineer Josh Wardle.

they are in. It may not always be obvious how they're feeling, but there are certain things that may give you a clue. For instance, when your colleagues are stressed, they may be far less chatty. People who are hunched over their keyboards frowning rather than leaning back in their office chair may not be in a relaxed state – they're either very absorbed or possibly anxious. Someone who isn't relaxed won't invite conversation by looking up at others in the office, they'll just be focused on their work, possibly staring hard at their computer screen or into space. People tapping their chin or their mouth and/or gazing upwards might well be lost in thought.

If they don't seem to be in a relaxed mood, wait until they are engaging more with the people around them again, or their posture is more leaning back than hunched. And if you're not sure, ask 'Is this a good time to talk about...?' Or, if there's someone in the office you trust, you could ask them whether they think it's a good time to approach someone you suspect may be feeling under pressure.

If you do really need to approach someone who has made it known they're stressed about something at work, you could make a comment that shows you are aware of it, like: 'Sorry to add to your troubles, but...'

TOP TIP: AVOID THE MOOD QUIZ

If you're not sure whether someone is angry or not, it's best not to ask them repeatedly if they're in a bad mood. Maura can testify to this being a sure-fire way to get them in a bad mood even if they weren't in one to start with.

A lot of autistics are hypersensitive to the mood in a room. If this is you, please don't assume you're the reason someone is in bad form or that you have to take personal responsibility for the welfare of everyone around you.

The hot air balloon

Because non-autistic people have this unspoken rule that they have to be professional and polite at all times at work, it does mean that any feelings of irritation and annoyance tend to be stored up.

People at work do mask quite a lot, especially when dealing with those that they don't personally like very much. We all know how draining masking can be!

It's completely normal for a team member to 'let off steam' (vent) by ranting to trusted colleagues about someone else they are working with. The best bet is to let them complain until the hot air they have stored up is released.

Keeping it zipped

One of the best lessons we've learnt from office life is not to share information that someone else tells you privately. Showing that you can be trusted builds great relationships. (Unless they confess to battering a cupcake thief to death with the blue stapler, in which case you should probably alert the authorities.) This means that if someone has been a bit rude about a colleague or customer whilst feeling annoyed, they are rather banking on the fact that you won't be sharing their views to the wider world.

Also, if someone privately tells you they are also autistic, keep it to yourself, even if you feel that it will make others more flexible towards them. In addition, if you suspect that someone else is autistic, it's best not to tell others (or the person concerned) your theory. Leave the choice to them.

It's a secret if they say...

- 'I want this to go no further'.
- 'This is for your ears only'.
- 'Off the record...'
- 'This hasn't been made public yet but...'
- 'Confidentially speaking...'

All of the above are phrases for 'Keep it zipped' (keep it to yourself).

It's a bore, but don't skip a chore

Part of being in an office team is sharing the burden of jobs no one likes much. If people take turns to empty the kitchen bin, clean the fridge, or wipe up the dishes, make sure you do your bit. It can be a bit annoying when someone constantly seems to avoid those jobs.

Card signings

Office teams often buy a joint birthday card for a colleague's birthday, signed by all members of the team. Non-autistics are really uptight about keeping a group card a secret until the big day. So if it's your turn to sign the card and you suddenly see the birthday boy/girl/non-binary person coming back to the desk, hide it! Put it in a drawer or under a pile of paper. Then try and look innocent.

The 'whip round' or gift collection

As you'll no doubt recall, a 'kitty' is the name for a joint cash collection of any sort. If the collection is for a gift, it may be referred to as a 'whip round'.

A 'whip round' happens if someone is collecting for a colleague's birthday or leaving gift. Nothing to do with Indiana Jones,[2] sorry. Everyone donates some cash and the total is spent on a nice gift from everyone at the office. Usually, the purchasing of a joint gift falls to the person in the office most excited about the prospect of going shopping when they should be working.

TOP TIP: THEY EXPECT YOU TO JOIN IN

The question 'Do you want to put anything in the kitty for Donna's birthday?' isn't really a question, although it sounds like one. We're afraid it is generally frowned upon if you give the searingly honest reply: 'No, I hate her guts'. Being a team player means a small donation for special occasions, although how small is up to you.

If you're not sure how much cash is appropriate to give towards a gift, just ask: 'How much are people putting in?'

Gifts are always a surprise, and whip rounds are always done in secret. Don't tell the recipient that the team is buying them a present. You'll give away the surprise, and this may be the most excitement the team has had all year... ☺.

---

2   Indiana Jones is an American action-adventure film hero whose hat and bullwhip are important parts of the character, played by Harrison Ford.

CHAPTER 8

WORKING RELATIONSHIPS

We discussed – okay, talked at you – before about being part of a team. This chapter goes into a bit more depth on individual and group interactions.

The name game

These days, using people's first names is fine, with very few exceptions. However, people can be fussy when it comes to getting their names right.

Just to use ourselves as an example, Debby has developed a distain for anyone who decides to shorten her name to 'Debs' or 'Deb' without knowing her well. To her this sounds like downright cheek and a little over-familiar (snort!).

And, watch for that vein throbbing in Maura's neck if you dare to call her 'Mo'. She's fighting the urge to whop you over the head with a frying pan. It's a bit like meeting King Charles III and saying 'Alright, Charlie?'

The solution is simple... and this calls for a top tip.

> ## TOP TIP: INTRODUCE YOURSELF FIRST
> Introduce yourself first, then the other person is obliged to do the same, and this way you'll know what they like to be called.

If in doubt, leave out any shortened forms. For instance, if Margaret wanted you to call her 'Mags' she would have no doubt said 'Just call me Mags' when you called her Margaret.

By the way, make sure people get *your* name right from the get go. There are folks out there who still think of Maura as Moira, Monica, Morag or even Mark (her voice sounds quite deep over the phone). And all because she didn't correct them the first time and the longer it went on the more awkward it became to say something.

Some tips:

- Be aware that people might be given nicknames by others which aren't supposed to be used in public or in front of them. If in doubt, leave it out.

- Making up your own nicknames for people is inadvisable unless you've known them for a long time and you're pretty sure they'll be okay with it.

The hinters

Not everyone is as direct, honest and open as autistic people. Life would be a lot easier if they were. Some people are a bit afraid of being critical, or creating conflict, and so they hint if they are unhappy with something rather than saying it outright. They may even make a little joke about it and leave you thinking 'Huh?'

Quick example: Mary didn't like it when Fiona left some work for her to complete on her desk. She said 'I see you've left a little present for me', which sounded like a light-hearted joke, but she didn't seem too happy. Fiona wasn't sure whether Mary was trying to tell her something. Would Mary rather she hadn't left it on her desk?

This is a bit rubbish, as autistic people sometimes aren't great at picking up on hints. If someone seems a bit unhappy but isn't being direct with you, or is joking in a way that implies some criticism, you could ask them outright, in a friendly way: 'Are you trying to tell me something, here? I'm not great at hints'.

Colleague or friend?

Non-autistics give off so many confusing social signals that at times it's virtually impossible to tell apart someone who is simply being a nice colleague from someone who is being a friend.

Most people at the office will be polite and approachable towards you. Non-autistics generally put a very high value on being friendly at work, as it makes them feel more comfortable and makes working together easier.

Fine. Fantastic.

However, most of the population are great pretenders. They're obsessed with social ease. It's so high up on their agenda that sometimes they'll mask negative reactions and be friendly and jokey with people who they privately love about as much as a cold bath in the middle of a snowstorm. If someone won't admit to your face that you're not their kind of person, it can be rather confusing.

How can you tell, then, whether someone is not just a colleague being superficially friendly, but also a friend?

We can feel some more tips coming on...

Tip 1: Colleagues first, friendships second

If you hunt down friendships as a priority, you may end up being a little over-familiar too soon. Real friendships take a long time to develop. It's best to keep to general topics of conversation rather than any great detail on your personal life. Over time, you may find this changes as others reveal slightly more about themselves. But don't rush it. The more you have in common other than the nature of your work, the more likely you will be to develop a genuine friendship.

Tip 2: Great colleagues are just as fun
Great colleagues are better than rubbish friends, so you needn't spend time outside work with them to really enjoy their company. Many people have quite stringent home/work boundaries and keep those two aspects of their lives completely separate. This means that no tensions outside of work ever affect their ability to function well inside the office or at work.

Tip 3: Too much too soon?
If someone has turned down your social invitation, don't assume they don't like you. They may be genuinely busy, or it could be a case that they just don't feel they know you well enough. They don't say this out loud, of course. That would make life FAR too easy.

Tip 4: Go easy on the romantic overtures
Sorry to spell this out, but be careful not to approach anyone in the office for a romantic date unless you are 100% certain that it is appropriate and they would welcome it. If you get it wrong, it's pretty disastrous and embarrassing for your working life. At best, you'll be the subject of gossip – it always seems amusing to others when someone gets an awkward romantic knock-back. At worst, your unwelcome offer could be seen as harassment, whether it's to a woman, a man or someone non-binary. Better to be safe than sorry, as they say.

Of course, this could happen the other way around too – Maura once found herself on an accidental date since she's rubbish at picking up on those sorts of cues – in which case think carefully about whether you want to reciprocate your co-worker's romantic overtures. If not, it's preferable to remain on good terms with them, unless they are persistent or harassing you. In this case, talk to your manager or Human Resources department and see Chapter 10.

Tip 5: Stick to safe topics
If you're the only one sharing the more intimate aspects of your life – such as details about your family or relationships, or your insecurities and anxieties – that's not a friendship, that's having a counselling session. True friendships are usually based on people getting to know each other properly over time.

Tip 6: Wait till you're asked
If you're not sure whether someone is more a friend than a colleague, you could wait until they ask you to do something outside of work with them. Work outings with a group of colleagues don't necessarily mean they are your friends, but if someone wants to do something socially with just you that's unconnected with work, there's a potential friendship. Usually people start becoming friends at work when they find they have more in common than just being work colleagues, such as sharing an interest in the same music or sports.

Tip 7: Trust people who are direct
Fortunately, some non-autistics have more than a touch of autistic honesty and can't be bothered playing mind games. They'll be friendly but also direct. When they have to make a criticism, it will be to another person's face, not behind their back. They will be the one to point out to you (kindly, we hope) if you've misunderstood any office etiquette. This doesn't necessarily mean they are your buddy, but it does mean that if they are kind with their guidance, you should be able to ask questions and get an honest response.

Tip 8: It's not just about venue

Working lunches and after-work drinks with colleagues may be social, but these guys *still* don't qualify as close friends just because the hour is after 5pm and the place is a pub. Even outside work, your colleagues may still steer away from discussing their most private thoughts. This doesn't mean you can't enjoy their company but avoid giving too much away about your private life. No divulging details of your last break-up...

When it goes wrong...

Jenny is delighted when Pam is friendly to her at work. After a few days, she asks Pam if she'd like to come to see a film with her. Pam is a bit taken aback, she doesn't know Jenny that well and was just being welcoming. She makes an excuse and says she's busy, and she doesn't talk to Jenny as much in case Jenny assumes there's a real friendship and asks again.

Jenny didn't do anything wrong, but she was a bit over-familiar too soon. Most colleagues stick to working relationships unless they have quite a deep connection with someone else. (Just as well she didn't break Pam's mug too. Sheesh.)

Joining in conversations

Conversation aimed at everyone including you is:

- at a volume that everyone can hear. The speaker will also be looking at people sitting at other desks that are more than one person away from them. Or, they might be standing in a group that is spaced apart, rather than in a smaller huddle

- talking about a very general subject, such as hobbies or work in general, rather than something very specific

- making eye contact with everyone, including you if you're looking attentively at them.

For private chat you shouldn't join in, watch for these signs:

- Two speakers are huddled quite close together, their bodies pointing towards each other, not the group. This means the chat is just between them.

- You may be able to catch some of the conversation, but it's certainly not loud.

- The topic seems to be of a more personal nature.

- If you're looking attentive, no eye contact is made with you.

If you aren't sure whether to join in, wait to be asked your opinion on something, or you could ask directly: 'Is this a private chat? I wouldn't want to intrude'.

Ready for some real-life examples?

No, we don't like boring case studies either, as they remind us of office training videos in the 1980s starring John Cleese,[1] where every example was deeply obvious and a bit patronizing (by today's standards). Hopefully, however, you'll forgive us for imagining a few situations typical of the sorts you'll come across, and observing where things go well and not so well.

---

1 The company Video Arts was founded by comic actor John Cleese to help inject some humour into workplace learning. It's still producing humorous training videos today.

Story 1

Pat is typing away opposite Judy and Paul, who sit next to each other in a group of desks. They've turned towards each other and are talking about what they did at the weekend.

Pat interrupts: 'I went to see *Dancing on Ice* on Saturday!'

They both look up and say 'Nice', and then they carry on their own chat.

They might have seemed rude, but the two were talking to each other quite close together, so were having a private chat. When the flow of conversation was interrupted, they weren't that welcoming of a new topic.

Story 2

John walks into a meeting room where some of his colleagues are standing in a group, at a distance of a few feet from each other. Some of them are getting coffee and others are chatting about sport.

John walks up to the group and listens patiently for a bit. Martin turns to him and asks, 'Which team do you support?' John says, 'I don't really support a team, I'm more of a video games person than into sport'.

John doesn't interrupt a chat that has already started, but he can see that people are spaced slightly apart and chatting quite loudly, not privately, so he stands with them for a bit. Since he hasn't interrupted, he isn't disrupting the flow of conversation and the group willingly includes him. He also manages to turn the conversation away from sport and onto something he's more comfortable talking about.

Story 3

Jamie is the first into a meeting room when a few more of his colleagues arrive and start making the tea. 'Did anyone else see that documentary on BBC1 last night?' Jamie asks them. 'Oh yeh, the one on car crime?' replies Nancy. 'It was good, wasn't it?'

Instead of starting off with 'I watched a documentary last night...' Jamie asks the others whether they saw it. This means that he doesn't end up explaining what it is about to anyone who did see it, and he's immediately involved other people.

Our topmost tip here, though, is something it took both of us years to figure out.

Ready?

You don't have to make everyone like you.

Some people will like you and some people will not, and that's okay. You won't like everyone you meet either. Nobody is liked by everyone. Well, with the possible exception of Pedro Pascal.[2]

A harmonious office depends on people being pleasant around each other but that's not the same as people-pleasing. What other people think of you is their business and not your responsibility.

As we've said before – and we will keep saying it – you do not have to change who you are or pretend to be somebody else.

---

2   A popular Chilean-American actor.

CHAPTER 9

OFFICE GOSSIPS

Okay, so you've figured out when to join in on the office chat. This next bit is about some things to watch out for so you don't end up in an uncomfortable situation at work. First up is how to spot and deal with office gossips.

The difference between gossip and banter

Gossip is different to banter. Banter is face-to-face chatter, and a bit like a verbal sport, where people make jokey comments to each other and expect to get them back in return (more on this in the next chapter).

Gossip is about people who aren't present. On one level, it can just be agreeing that you think a colleague or client is difficult or demanding in some way. People do that a lot! It's part of that hot air balloon exercise of releasing tension by sharing your feelings of exasperation we talked (at you) about in Chapter 7.

On a more damaging level, gossip can mean talking about more private matters behind someone's back. This can include mistakes they've made at work or relationships they've had with others either inside or outside of work.

Why do people indulge in office gossip, that is talking about people who work at the same organization?

The answer is simple enough. Small talk about TV is all very well, but there's nothing non-autistics like better than talking about other people and dramas closer to home.

Hence gossip.

Gossip can be as harmless as the news that Stacey from accounts is going out with Graeme from marketing.

Or it can be as harmful as the news that married Stacey from accounts is having an affair with married Graeme from marketing.

Negative as it seems, there is a purpose to office gossip. Like small talk, it's a bonding exercise.

Also, remember our hot air balloon analogy, about people having to vent their frustration? Well, if you're all in agreement that someone is very hard to deal with, and you are able to chat about it, it gives people a sense of reinforcement. If they come across conflict at work, people can feel very insecure about themselves, and chatting about the other person being difficult can help them to ease their own anxieties.

Now, look. We aren't saying that it's nice or particularly professional to gossip about others. We *definitely* aren't saying you should start off the gossip yourself.

However, don't feel obliged to call people out when they do it. Unless you feel that the gossip is deeply cruel and harmful to a person's reputation, you're usually best not to say anything. You don't have to join in with it.

Tips on dealing with office gossip:

Tip 1: Don't be the instigator

Don't ever be the person to start talking about someone else behind their back. As the source of gossip, if you're found out for it you could be in for a confrontation from the person themselves or a close pal of theirs.

It's also wise to be aware that both e-mails and platforms like Zoom and Teams are considered work communication and so it's best not to moan about someone on any of them – or participate in any gossip.

Tip 2: Be careful how you challenge gossip
If you think a piece of gossip is unwarranted, you may be tempted to say: 'I don't think that's very professional', which might be true but could aggravate a colleague. What you could say instead is: 'Where did you hear that?' Questioning the source of their gossip will help others to assess its reliability and give out the message that you're not prepared to accept unsubstantiated gossip about someone without question.

If you don't think the gossip is very reliable or fair, you can say 'I'm not sure I believe that'. What you're doing here is diluting the strength of the story and helping to counter it without getting into a direct argument with someone. Without saying it, you're making it clear that you won't be spreading that gossip.

TOP TIP: NEVER TELL A GOSSIPER YOUR SECRETS

If they gossip *to* you, you can be damned sure they'll gossip *about* you. So don't tell them anything you wouldn't want to see displayed on the side of a bus. Most people are not great at keeping secrets, with the exception of trusted colleagues who respect their team's confidentiality. So be very careful before you share anything private with your work colleagues.

If you know you're personally being gossiped about all the time and isolated as a result, that's bullying and is covered in the next chapter.

CHAPTER 10

BANTER VERSUS BULLYING

M ost people you work with are likely to be nice – but here are some pointers for the rare situations when you find that someone isn't. If you like, only read this chapter if you do hit a problem.

Harmless versus hurtful banter

Kidding around and taking the mickey out of (making fun of) others is what's known as 'office banter' or (if you're English and trying to sound like you're 'down with the kids') 'bants'.

Banter is very common in the office world, as it offers a bit of humour and light relief to the setting without people having to get into deep discussions.

If everyone joins in the banter and you're included, you should take it as a friendly sign, providing the jokes aren't overtly cruel. Gently taking the mickey out of someone can be a sign that they like you enough to relax around you.

Usually, people do think about it before they aim banter at you. If they feel you're a sensitive type, they are less likely to joke with you.

The people who get a lot of banter aimed at them are generally deemed to have a great sense of humour, be quite robust and not easily offended. Plus they can usually 'dish it out' as well (i.e. fling some banter back in the other person's direction).

If you are the sole target of the jokes, however, and you feel uncomfortable about it, have a word in private. More on that later.

Example of office banter

Clive: Don't ask Mike about anything this morning, he's not in a fit state.

Dan: Mike, were you out again last night?

Mike: Groaannnn. Yeh.

Clive: He's had to change pubs now, he's chatted up all the women in The Horse and Cart and there's none left.

Everyone laughs.

Mike: Yeh and I couldn't go to The Farrier because Clive's already scared off all the women from there.

Clive: Yeh that's true, there's only the 84-year-old one in the corner who still talks to me.

Mike may well have chatted up a few women, not all of them, and this is likely to be a massive exaggeration for the sake of humorous banter. In isolation, as long as Mike is okay with this kind of joking and robust enough to take it without sobbing quietly to himself that everyone thinks he's a womanizer, it's all in good humour. You can generally tell whether someone's enjoying banter aimed at them because they'll laugh and smile and be quite chatty back.

A line might be crossed if Mike doesn't find this funny or is ALWAYS the target and no one else is. But in our example, he's taken the joke okay and thrown a joke back in Clive's direction, which Clive also doesn't seem to mind. The two-way nature of the banter shows that they are both comfortable with it.

Bullying and harassment

We're going to have to level with you here: these next sections will not be humorous. Bullying and harassment are no laughing matter.

First, you need to know that as an employee, you are protected from bullying by law. Because of this, your organization is obliged to have policies that show how they are meeting the requirements of the law. More about that later.

What the law says

Under workplace health and safety law, employers have a duty to ensure the health, safety and welfare of their employees. Equality legislation also means that anyone with what's known as a 'protected characteristic', such as a disability,[1] has the right to be treated fairly and feel safe at work. Under these laws, your employer is also obliged to give you a fair chance at your role by making reasonable adjustments for you.

If someone is singling you out for less favourable treatment because you are autistic, or you feel humiliated, scared or upset, then by UK law this counts as discrimination.

The difference between banter and bullying

Now that you know you're protected from bullying, let's define what that is. We'll revisit the same 'banter' we showed earlier, but on this occasion, Mike is not enjoying the exchange.

1   As we mentioned earlier, you may not identify as disabled, but autistic people are considered to have a 'protected characteristic' by law.

> ### Example of 'banter' turned bullying
>
> Clive: Don't ask Mike about anything this morning, he's not in a fit state.
>
> Dan: Mike, were you out again last night?
>
> Mike: I did go out, yes.
>
> Clive: He's had to change pubs now, he's chatted up all the women in The Horse and Cart and there's none left.
>
> *Everyone laughs apart from Mike.*
>
> Mike: No, I wasn't chatting up any women.
>
> Clive: Ah yeh, that's what you say.
>
> Mike (crossly): I *wasn't* chatting up any women. I was there with my dad.
>
> Clive: There with your dad, yeh. Bet he was stalking the ladies as well. (*Sarcastically*) Double the charm offensive!
>
> *Everyone laughs apart from Mike.*
>
> Mike: Why would you say that? My dad is faithful to my mum. And he would never stalk anyone because that's horrible, not to mention illegal.

In the example above, Clive has chosen to banter with Mike, who doesn't see the funny side of being accused of chatting up women when he had no intention of doing so.

And yup, Clive does seem a bit childish. Once Mike has given 'back off' signals, showing he doesn't appreciate the conversation, Clive doesn't take the hint. He continues to make the same joke, digging deeper for a response – and he even brings Mike's dad into it.

The law is fairly straightforward when it comes to harassment. If you feel as if you are being harassed, then the other person should stop. Harassment isn't defined by *what* they say, but *how* you are responding to it.

Jokes aimed at you: If you find a jokey conversation offensive or uncomfortable, the person should zip it (stop), pronto. If they refuse to, and keep going despite your obvious discomfort, repeatedly, then you may need to do something about it.

Maybe we'd give Clive the benefit of the doubt and assume he was mistaken during this conversation. He's learnt his lesson, right? The lesson is: don't pick on Mike, he doesn't find it funny.

If he repeatedly had that kind of conversation knowing that it wasn't appreciated, then this amounts to bullying. If we've crossed someone's comfort boundary and we know it, we're to blame.

If someone is verbally abusive to you, makes jokes or uses sarcasm at your expense or does cruel impersonations... you don't have to put up with it. This applies whether or not their behaviour is anything to do with you being autistic.

Before you get too worried, most people are enlightened enough not to do this. We'd be very disappointed if you came across it. Bullying at work is well recognized as unacceptable. Unlike school, if there happens to be a bit of a jerk in the office, someone else often puts them right, especially if you confide to a trusted colleague that you're feeling uncomfortable. Responsible team members just won't put up with it.

However, if you start to dread coming into work because someone is deliberately making life difficult for you, and if no one has yet pointed out to them that they should zip it, then as we've said, you need to do something about it.

Anti-bullying policies

As required by the laws mentioned earlier, organizations have policies designed to protect their employees from bullying and stating clearly what steps will be taken should it occur. These policies are your protective shield and should stop anyone from even thinking about it in the first place!

The policy that covers bullying might just be called 'Bullying Policy' or it's sometimes described as a 'Dignity at Work' policy. Bullying policies are designed to address a pattern of repeatedly unacceptable behaviour.

If what's happened to you is a one-off incident, it may fall under the organization's Grievance Policy instead.

The policies should tell you how to raise a complaint and should be easily accessible to all employees online.

So, if you're experiencing some form of harassment or bullying, what should you do?

1. Chat to a colleague

First, you might want to chat to colleagues to find out whether they witnessed the treatment and if they also felt that it was bullying or harassment. Maybe they've been subjected to it themselves. You might be able to tackle this together.

2. If you can, approach the person

Second, if (possibly having discussed this with others) you feel that this person could be approached directly and that the behaviour is based on ignorance, you could simply point out to them that you know they didn't intend to upset you, but that you'd rather they stopped.

A colleague might well be prepared to approach the other person for you, but if you can muster the courage to mention it yourself, it's less likely to reoccur.

3. Make an informal complaint to your manager

If you've tried to resolve this yourself and your remarks are brushed aside, your distress minimized or you just feel as if you're getting nowhere, you can step it up a notch by making an informal complaint. This usually just involves talking to your manager.

Before you make a complaint: Before you raise a complaint with anyone, start gathering evidence as soon as possible. Keep any messages about the problem and write some notes of what happened. Keep e-mails and retain screenshots of anything sent about you (including the date), as well as social media posts and messages. Log any verbal comments or physical behaviour that might count as bullying or harassment.

Nine times out of ten, your direct manager should be able to resolve this for you. No one wants an unhappy crew member. If your manager isn't helpful, or indeed it's the manager who is the problem, you may need to go to your manager's boss or to your Human Resources department, if you have one, for advice.

A real-life example

Debby once had a very difficult manager who upset ALL his employees with his overly demanding and bullying demeanour. As a senior member of her team, she raised a grievance with her boss's boss, who took her evidence on board and worked hard to resolve the issue. Her boss still had all the diplomacy skills of a bouquet of flowers walking into a support group for hay fever sufferers, but he did improve slightly.

4. Tell your union, if you have one

Larger organizations, in particular in the public service, may also have a union you can join. Unions are official organizations forged to protect employees' rights at work, so it's worth joining one if you're offered the chance (there's generally an annual fee). If you tell a union about the issue, there will be a representative assigned to help you to resolve the problem.

Unions can support you as you navigate your way through a complaints procedure, which can take quite some time, attend meetings with you related to your complaint or talk on your behalf to Human Resources.

5. Approach an outside agency, like the Citizen's Advice Bureau

Finally, if no one else is helping you and you feel as if you need support, you could look up the telephone line mentioned in the support section at the end of the book, or in the UK you can contact the Citizen's Advice Bureau online, which gives free advice.

If you don't feel that the organization is handling your complaint well, under what are known as 'labour relations procedures' a mediator could come in from outside of the organization to help both you and your employer reach an agreement. More about that in the support section at the end of the book.

6. Make a formal complaint

So, you've tried all of these suggestions and things still aren't resolved. Honestly, we'd be surprised if you got to this point, but it's not unheard of, so let's plough on! As we mentioned earlier, your organization's policies should tell you how to go about making a formal complaint. This is a big step, though, so it really is best to make sure you've done whatever you can to resolve the matter informally first. Be aware that an allegation does not count as evidence and you're likely to need to provide details of people who witnessed any incidents and/or written materials to support your complaint. Do not assume that witnesses will want to go on the record – how much they are willing to say is for them to decide – or that they will completely agree with your version of events.

7. Quit or take legal action against the organization

The very last resort is taking legal action against the organization. If you need to do it, some helpful contacts are also written in Support for you in the workplace at the end of the book.

Some people just don't want to stay and fight because of the effects on their mental health, and you can hardly blame them. They quit instead. If you told your organization you were unhappy and why, and you exhausted their internal procedures, you might be able to claim what's called constructive dismissal.

This is when you've been forced to quit a role because of your organization's treatment of you and you could get compensated if there is evidence that their treatment of you was unfair. Bear in mind, though, that there are no guarantees you will win your case and if you lose you could be liable for legal costs. There are some organizations, like the Equality Commission (if you're in the UK), who may be able to support you in taking a case against your employer.

> **Victimization:** If you do stay, and your employer does something that disadvantages you or you're not happy about just because you made a complaint – for instance, moving you to another role without your agreement – that may qualify as 'victimization'. There are protections against this in law as well.

That was a very brief outline to show you that you don't have to suffer in silence. Our best advice is not to go it alone – find an advisor who can support you.

What if *you* end up being accused of bullying or harassment?

Nobody likes to be accused of inappropriate behaviour, especially if they feel the accusation is unfair. It may be that you said something to somebody intending it as a joke and they got upset, even though that wasn't your intention. But here's the thing: bullying is in the eye of the beholder. In other words, if someone is genuinely hurt by something you said or did, it may be seen as inappropriate even if it wasn't your intention to upset them.

Our advice? If you upset someone, apologize for it as soon as you're made aware of this. We don't mean a half-hearted apology, like 'I'm sorry if you were offended'. We mean something far more remorseful, like 'I am genuinely sorry I upset you. I hope you can accept that I didn't mean to and that I will be more careful in future so that this doesn't happen again'.

Most people should be happy with a genuine apology. However, if they're not, or if you believe the accusation is genuinely un-founded or even completely untrue, our advice is to talk to some-one and seek help. If you're a member of a staff union, they can help you whether you're the person making a complaint or the one being complained against. And your manager and Human Resources also have a responsibility for your wellbeing, too.

For more information and advice, have a look at the further reading and support sections at the end of this book.

CHAPTER 11

MEETINGS

and how to stay awake in them

Many workplaces have regular team catch-ups, either in person or using remote links. Meetings have a habit of being rather dull if the conversation focuses for some minutes on something that doesn't affect you at all.

First things first, you may need something to fiddle with to keep focused in a meeting. If anyone asks, you can just say that a fidget helps you to focus. If you're in a virtual meeting, you won't need to explain to anyone about fidgets as they won't be able to see them, ha ha.

You'll find that non-autistics also stim during meetings, though sometimes in more subtle ways, like tapping pens, fiddling with hair or doodling. When forced to sit still and listen, we're all trying to self-regulate to one degree or another. The difference is that non-autistics are usually trying to wake themselves up with fidgeting, whereas for autistic folks it's more often about trying to calm down an over-active brain.

Either way, no one loves a meeting.

Meeting preliminaries

Don't ask us why, maybe it's their obsession with all things social, but non-autistic people are incapable of starting a meeting without 'social niceties'. So, whether it's two or twenty people, you'll find there's likely to be some small talk to navigate before you get to the point.

If the meeting is in an office, you may be asked if you want tea or coffee before it starts. It's an unwritten rule in some offices that no meeting can possibly be conducted without the offer of a hot drink.

As we've said before, it's a great idea to learn how to make tea and coffee even if you don't drink them yourself, just in case you invite someone to your own meeting. It makes people feel comfortable if they've got a warm mug to hold onto, a bit like a sensory toy we suppose. Don't despair if you can't make drinks and don't want to, just lead them to the kettle/vending machine and ask if they'd like to help themselves to a drink.

If you're stuck for pre-meeting chat, just ask the person you're sitting nearest how things are going.

Agendas

You'll probably like this bit: most official meetings come with an agenda prepared in advance. Just in case you've never come across one before, an agenda is simply a list of all the things to be discussed in the meeting, in the order in which they are to be discussed. How very autism-friendly! 'AOB' at the bottom of an agenda means 'any other business' and is designed to cover anything you want to alert people to (work-wise) that hasn't been mentioned earlier.

If you have anything of major importance to discuss that relates to the meeting being held, it's better to ask the person arranging the meeting to add it to the agenda. AOB is really just for small extras.

The chair

No, we don't mean the piece of furniture you sit on during the meeting, though you will probably need one of those too. What we're talking about here is the person leading the meeting (although if they're not very good at it, they may seem quite wooden as well). They used to be called the 'chairman', back in the days when being in a position of authority required you to have a Y chromosome. That morphed into 'chairperson' but often it's just 'chair' nowadays.

If you get a bit bored, feel free to imagine it's a talking chaise longue taking you through the agenda.

Introductions

If the people in your meeting haven't all met before, the meeting is likely to start with introductions. People tell the others present their name and role, nothing more is needed. Don't worry if you can't remember everyone's name and role, you can always ask for a reminder from someone when they speak during the meeting if you're not sure (and everyone else will be relieved, as they will have forgotten, too).

Most meetings do not last longer than an hour and they aren't like school. You do not have to put up your hand to go to the toilet during a meeting. Just say, 'Excuse me a moment', and leave the room. Nor do you have to put up your hand to make a point (assuming the meeting is in person), although a raised index finger can be helpful to inform the chair that you'd like to say something. Reaching for the sky shouting 'Me, me me! PICK ME!' for ten minutes is generally frowned upon, though.

Introducing your thought

Before saying anything relevant to the point being discussed, if you aren't asked directly for your view, it's a great idea to say: 'Can

I just add something?' This means that rather than barging in with a point, you've got the others ready for it first.

TOP TIP: FLAGGING

Offering one line to suggest what you want to raise helps you to focus your thoughts and it also means that everyone else orientates quickly. Many people don't bother doing it, but it's impressive when you do. For example, 'Just a point about what's in the press release you're about to send...' or 'Regarding the design that you just spoke about, I have a question'.

At this point, the chair of the meeting may either say 'Go ahead' or may indicate that your views could be saved for a different section of the meeting.

We recommend you always take a notepad to a meeting. Use notes to remind yourself of what you want to mention later on or when someone has finished speaking.

How do you shut them up?

If you are meeting with someone who is giving you way too much information too quickly, you can ask them to slow down a bit or follow up in writing. Never feel shy of asking: 'Can I just check what that means?' or 'Sorry – could you repeat what you just said again?' Asking for clarification is reasonable and often necessary.

If you are in charge of a meeting and you feel that someone is dominating it by talking too much, you can simply say, 'Okay, thank you for that', whilst they're talking and then add: 'I'd like to bring Janice (for example) into this, now. What do you think, Janice?' So, you can actually shut a person up by thanking them and inviting someone else to speak if you feel that they aren't getting a chance to offer their view.

One of Debby's former managers used to use hand signals at meetings, a bit like a traffic officer. He'd gently hold up a hand to stop someone from talking whilst his other hand waved another speaker 'forward' – 'What do you think?' It was highly effective.

When visitors come for meetings

Visitors to the organization can be really important, since they are capable of advertising it to others, or smashing its reputation to bits, depending on their impression of your office.

If a potential client or important contact is to visit the office for a meeting with you, you may need to dress slightly smarter that day. Business people love a good old-fashioned handshake as a greeting so don't be surprised if they stick out their hand faster than a cowboy whips out his gun in a Western shoot-out. If you don't want to shake hands, avoiding contact needn't be awkward. You can be equally welcoming with something like: 'Sorry I don't do handshakes, but good to meet you. Come in, have a seat...'

Try to avoid mentioning that you're overtired, underpaid, and the company boss drives you up the wall, across the ceiling and down the other side (really annoys you).

In fact, try and avoid sharing grievances about anyone in your organization, either inside or outside the meeting, even if the visitor is someone who seems instantly on your wavelength.

Similarly, bear in mind that anything to do with the cash a private company is earning, or any of its difficulties as a business, should also be very much secret squirrel (kept confidential). Keep private company details under wraps.

In short, be loyal to your organization even if privately you have concerns about it. Nice as the visitors may be, you never know who they are going to share the information with.

Great tips for staying alert in a meeting:

Tip 1: Show them that you're listening

Looking at a person who is speaking during a meeting can be quite hard, especially if you're trying to process what they're saying or they're droning on a bit. A glance every now and then is enough, and an occasional small nod will show you're awake. Nodding whilst not listening at all is inadvisable, as you may find that you've just appeared pleasantly chuffed at the company's disastrous loss of a major client.

Making notes is ideal even if you don't use them afterwards. They show that you are being attentive without having to stare at someone's eyeballs for lengthy periods of time.

Subtle doodling is generally accepted, but the darker sort that depicts arrows and small missiles being aimed in the speaker's direction should probably be kept inside your head in case someone else, equally bored, peers over your shoulder.

Tip 2: Avoid displaying bored body language

The temptation to rest your head on your arms during a meeting and have a nice long nap can be overwhelming. You may well be bored out of your flipping mind, but try to avoid loud sighs, puffing your cheeks, yawning, stretching or closing your eyes. This is considered rude and unprofessional, even if deeply enticing.

It's especially important to stay awake when there are guests from outside of the organization. If this means asking beforehand which part of the meeting you are required for – causing you to be present for a shorter amount of time – that's a tremendous win and you can even refer to it as a 'better use of my time'. This makes you look clever and cool rather than allergic to meetings.

Tip 3: The snacks shouldn't be more interesting than the meeting

Some organizations will put tempting biscuits or sweets out for a meeting.

TOP TIP: BISCUITS BEFOREHAND ARE BETTER

Before the meeting starts, offer the plate to the people sitting either side of you, let them take a biscuit, then help yourself to one or two of your favourites. It's preferable to do this early, not during the meeting.

Why? Why the heck put out biscuits if you don't want people to eat them during the meeting, eh?

The answer is, non-autistics like to look welcoming, and since most office environments are as dull as ditch water, a Jammie Dodger™ or two can really cheer a place up. However, it's really hard to look as if you're focused on what's being said whilst weighing up whether to pinch the last one or not.

Getting to the biscuits usually requires reaching or leaning over other people. If you're doing this more than once during a meeting, you're giving the certain impression that you're just here for the biscuits.

Now, we know that you probably are just here for the biscuits – but if you're too focused on them, it can start to appear less like a meeting and more like a picnic.

So, offer the biscuits around, take a couple, then leave well alone. That is, unless someone passes them to you during the meeting. In which case, make sure you always sit next to them in future – then your biscuit-deprivation days will be over.

CHAPTER 12

'ARE YOU A MATHS GENIUS?'

Talking to your colleagues about autism

B ack when the authors' kids were being assessed for autism, the biggest problem was that no one else knew what it was. The biggest problem nowadays is that everybody *thinks* they do. It's the perfect example of a little knowledge being a dangerous thing.

Telling other employees

Whether or not you share that you're autistic with your co-workers is up to you. You're very much not obliged to go around waving a placard announcing it.

However, as you get to know your colleagues, you might want to explain that certain sensory stimuli have an overwhelming effect on you, for instance. If you feel that you might need to go in a quiet room at certain times, or have a bit of a 'sensory' break with the agreement of your employer, it may be nice to explain why to co-workers.

You don't have to make it a big deal; just preparing people for the fact that you may occasionally disappear to regain focus should help them to understand. You don't have to say it's down to autism, of course, you can just mention sensory sensitivities and leave it at that.

This is deeply personal, though. Only say something if you feel it will help you.

Myths and misconceptions

Some people do have a good grasp of what autism is about, which is great, but many people think they understand more than they actually do. In the workplace, a number of your colleagues are likely to have heard a bit about autism because somebody in their extended family or a friend's kid has been professionally identified. Or, they watched a couple of episodes of *The Big Bang Theory*.

So don't be surprised if, after learning you're autistic (if you've chosen to tell them), some people immediately assume you're a maths or computer genius and try to adopt you as their personal Tech Support. (Just tell them to try switching it off and switching it on again.)

If we had a pound/euro/dollar for every time some well-meaning person asked us what our kiddo's 'special ability' was, we could stop buying lottery tickets. Even though it's only a minority of autistic people who have savant abilities, the idea of every autistic person having some sort of party trick has stuck, not helped by what we tend to see on film and TV. (Just tell them you have X-Ray vision.)

Others may speak to you very slowly with an exaggerated smile on their face like they're a greeter in the Disney Store. Now, to be clear, we're *not* saying you should be insulted to be mistaken for someone with an intellectual disability (and if anyone did say that, the vein in Maura's neck would start throbbing again). People born with intellectual and developmental disabilities (IDDs) or who have an acquired brain injury are as much a part of the neurodivergent

community as anybody else and are as entitled to be treated with dignity and respect.

But we totally get that it's frustrating to feel underestimated or presumed incompetent. It's frustrating for someone with IDD too, actually. The best way to put them right is by acing the job – let the quality of your work speak for itself. They'll soon catch on.

There may be those who tell you you're 'an inspiration' or 'very brave' for, well, existing. In an actual office. You may well be thinking 'I'm taking the minutes, not finding the cure for cancer, Trevor' but probably best not to say that out loud.

Then there's the 'autism deniers'. They may have different reasons for this – usually that you don't fit their stereotypical idea of what being autistic 'looks like' or, for a certain demographic, 'there was none of that in my day'. Or, they might be terrified that they themselves may have a case of the autismz – heaven forfend...

Maura once spent a 'fun' evening at a dinner party being told repeatedly she can't be autistic since all autistics are men. Her personal favourite, though, remains 'you can't be autistic, people like you!' People often see us as rare, exotic creatures and greatly underestimate how many autistic and otherwise neurodivergent people there are in the world.

It was only a joke!

Office banter is another one of those social bonding activities we mentioned earlier, and someone may think they're being funny if they call you 'Rain Man'[1], 'Sheldon'[2] or 'Saga' (a character from Scandi crime thriller *The Bridge*[3] in case you haven't seen it – we

---

1 A 1988 film starring Dustin Hoffman with an autistic savant as its protagonist.

2 Sheldon is a character from the comedy *The Big Bang Theory* (2007), widely assumed to be autistic.

3 A Scandinavian TV thriller set between Denmark and Sweden.

had to dig deep and consult an atlas to find an example of female autistic representation on the telly).

If both people are laughing, it's a joke. If the person who's the subject of the so-called joke isn't, the other one is being a bit of a dick. If someone is making you uncomfortable, you are well within your rights to ask them to stop ('Actually, I'd prefer it if you didn't call me that'). And, if they don't, you are well within your rights to speak to someone about it, as detailed in Chapter 10.

What should you do?

First and foremost, don't let other people's ignorance put you off. Try not to take it too personally: this is about them and their lack of knowledge, not you.

Ultimately, it's up to you how much you want to share with your co-workers about your lived experience or autism in general.

Do not feel obliged to carry the mental load of being an advocate for your entire neuroclan, but if you're comfortable talking to people about autism there are a few ways of going about it.

Try to respond to clueless questions positively, in a tone that suggests the question was perfectly understandable, not a load of rubbish. Rather than creating animosity, it's always better to ignore the ignorance and educate. That is, unless someone was deliberately being a dick and aiming to insult, see above.

You can keep it informal and just let people know you're autistic and that it's okay to ask questions. People may be nervous of doing that for fear of saying the wrong thing, so don't be surprised if tumbleweed blows across a silent office[4] following your invitation. That same nervousness can cause people to fall back on cringey

---

4   A metaphorical idiom suggesting that there's awkward silence for such a long time that you can hear tumbleweed blowing, like before a cowboy shoot-out. Yes, we probably have watched too many Westerns.

phrases like 'differently abled' or to claim they 'don't see disability'. (Resist the urge to tell them to go to Specsavers.[5])

If you're up for it, you could give a presentation. That may sound daunting, but people tend to find the topic really interesting and talking at people using a prepared script can actually be easier than a two-way conversation, since you are in control of the narrative. A bit of humour can put people at ease, not to mention smash yet another pesky stereotype – that autistic people can't have a sense of humour!

Or if you express yourself better in writing, you could draft or share a short article for the staff magazine or office intranet.

What's in a word?

If you've spent any time at all on social media, you will know that precision in language can mean a lot to autistic people.

Feelings can run high over such things as identity-first ('autistic') versus person-first ('person with autism') terminology. We use 'autistic' in this guide since most people who express a preference say they find this more respectful. There's also a vigorous debate about the proper usage of 'neurodiverse' and 'neurodivergent', whether it's okay to use 'Asperger Syndrome', 'on the spectrum', 'ASD', 'ASC' and so on.

The vast majority of the population is blissfully unaware of this sometimes heated discourse and will repeat whatever terminology they happen to have seen or heard.

If you feel the urge to correct someone, it's worth taking a beat.[6] Not everyone who uses terminology incorrectly does so out of malice. People generally mean well and are just being a bit

---

5   Specsavers Optical Group Ltd is a British multinational optical retail chain – optician to you and me.

6   Taking a moment to think.

clumsy in how they express themselves. Give them the benefit of the doubt unless and until they give you a solid reason to believe they're being derogatory or inappropriate, in which case you might want to take it to your line manager or someone in Human Resources. Maura recalls once being told 'he's a complete arsehole – totally on the spectrum' and having to give an impromptu TED talk[7] about why that's a load of tosh.

If someone slips up, they may be grateful to you for putting them straight or it could cause embarrassment, depending on the person and the situation. A gentle 'you might not know this, but most of us prefer...' in private will probably go down better than a public scolding (or 'roasting' as Debby's son would put it), which might make them claim they're being 'cancelled'.

Remember, you do not need to carry the full weight of educating the world about autism. To quote the great *Frozen*[8] prophetess Elsa, sometimes it's best to 'Let It Go'. If it helps, imagine her belting out the chorus at full throttle.

Explaining what works for you

You don't have to apologize for being you, nor are you obliged to explain any behaviour such as stimming or echolalia. However, sometimes it's not a bad thing to help others understand why something works for you, and possibly cause them to be less confused if it's unusual.

For instance, Debby's son Bobby was on the dentist chair when,

---

7   TED Conferences LLC is a non-profit media organization that posts international talks online for free distribution under the slogan 'ideas worth spreading'. 'TED talks' have become known for being short, informative and inspiring.

8   *Frozen* is a 2013 Disney film. Did you know that the song *Let It Go*, sung by Elsa in the film, was the ninth best-selling song of 2014 in the United States? No, we didn't either.

in answer to a question, he waved his hand around a bit. Before giving the answer to the dentist, he said: 'Sorry about that – that's just a bit of anxiety'. The dentist didn't need the explanation, and Bobby didn't have anything to apologize for, but it did help her to understand.

If you need to sit somewhere quietly for a bit, you can tell people 'Don't worry – not being anti-social – I just get a bit of sensory overload sometimes and need some quiet'. Or, when chewing gum: 'I find chewing gum really helps me to focus. Want one?'

People don't have an automatic right to know *why*, but if you're comfortable with just a small explanation here and there, they should feel more relaxed around you and will probably be a lot more understanding. As well as that, they'll feel more able to ask questions, since you've been volunteering information. The more they understand you, the more likely you are to have a smooth working relationship and a friendly advocate should an associate outside of your circle be less understanding. However, this is entirely up to you.

Common questions/statements and suggested responses

Question: Don't autistic people take things literally?

Tempting answer: No, that's a kleptomaniac. Ha ha ha. (With thanks to the person who originally came up with that joke. It wasn't us, but we haven't been able to find the source despite wanting to credit them).

Recommended answer: The literal meaning of something is the first thing that comes to mind, and sometimes we have to think a little longer if there's an abstract concept behind it.

Question: Will you always be autistic?

Tempting answer: (*Sarcastically*) No, autism magically disappears on your 21st birthday.

Recommended answer: Yes, it's part of who I am, just like blue eyes or brown hair.

———

Question: Are you good with numbers?

Tempting answer: Well done, you've watched *Rain Man*.

Recommended answer: That's a bit of a stereotype. It's true that lots of autistic people find numbers easy to deal with. But I'm afraid it's not true that autistic people are all good with numbers, it's just that you tend only to hear about the really gifted ones.

———

Question: Do you like that Greta Thunberg (or insert alternative celebrity) then? She's autistic.

Tempting answer: (*Sarcastically*) Yes, I love everyone who is autistic, just like you love everyone who wears glasses.

Recommended answer: I make up my mind about people as individuals whether or not they are autistic, it doesn't make a difference to me. I might understand them a little better, I guess.

———

Statement: Wow, I really admire people like you and how you cope.

Tempting answer: Coping with this kind of chat is a bit taxing, yeh.

Recommended answer: (*Do accept that they have made an effort here, even if it's a bit clumsy*). I've never known any different. People not understanding autism is the hard bit.

———

Statement: My neighbour's cousin's sister-in-law has autism.

Tempting answer: (*Sarcastically*) You mean there's more than one autistic person? Wow!

Recommended answer: It's much more common than you think.

———

Statement: Hopefully they'll cure autism one day.

Tempting answer: We don't need curing; other people need educating.

Recommended answer: I feel it would be much better if 'they' found better ways of supporting us.

———

Statement: You're nearly normal though!

Tempting answer: That's really not the compliment you think it is.

Recommended answer: I'm a normal autistic person, what's normal for us isn't the same as what's normal for you, but who's normal anyway?

———

Question: It's a really big spectrum though isn't it? You don't seem that autistic.

Tempting answer: Oh boy, where do I start...?

Recommended answer: Well, just like any sector of the population, we're all different.

CHAPTER 13

THE BEST OF BOTH WORLDS

What you need to know about hybrid working

These days, plenty of people enjoy the best of both worlds: they are based in the office for a few days a week and the rest of the time they work from home. Remote working is sometimes called a 'blended' or 'hybrid' approach and it has proved to be very popular with most people – being around colleagues when they need to collaborate, and working quietly in their own surroundings, too.

Before remote working was a possibility, you may have had to take a day off work to wait in for a delivery. For a thousand reasons just like this (well okay, not a thousand, probably about ten), it can help you to balance your work and home life better if you're not based full-time in an office.

Of course, remote working doesn't mean no longer communicating with your colleagues. Instead, it could well mean more of your time spent on virtual meetings, writing e-mails and on your mobile phone. Remote working has brought with it new ways of doing things and – yes, you've guessed it – yet another list of Things You're Just Meant to Know.

For these reasons, we felt it would be a good idea to dedicate a chapter to some tips that will help you with remote working. Oh, and our publisher asked us to.

Creating a workspace

At the risk of stating the bleeding obvious, you'll need a comfortable workspace at home, ideally some place quiet and free from distractions. If you're in a shared house, that may be trickier but you could try establishing some ground rules with your co-habitees, like keeping the noise down during working hours and not disturbing you during meetings or when you're working on something that requires you to concentrate. It might be an idea to wear a headset – and if this doesn't help you to focus any better, you can at least pretend to be Lady Gaga on your tea breaks.

If you're regularly working from home, your employer may ask you to complete a health and safety assessment. It may feel like form-filling for the sake of it, but it's actually important to ensure you have a safe working environment. Things to look out for include trailing wires or objects that might be a tripping hazard. Not sure what you do about the cat, though.

You should also be mindful of your physical comfort. Some employers will supply a proper desk and chair for you to use at home. Also, make sure you take screen breaks, as you should in any workplace setting.

If you need to keep papers at home – and your workplace allows for this – make sure you have somewhere secure to store them. Take particular care with people's personal information.

In some cases, you may need to check your house insurance policy covers you for working from home.

Workstyle agreements

Your employer might want you to complete an agreement confirming what your working pattern will be, including how much of your time will be spent working remotely. How fixed or flexible this might be will depend on business needs, though they should also take into account any reasonable adjustments that might be relevant. If you need specialized equipment or adjusted furniture, you might be able to have this replicated at home.

Setting boundaries

If you're not careful, working from home can end up feeling like living at work. If you don't have a daily commute to and from the office, it can be hard to know when you should finish for the day. It can be tempting to continue checking e-mails late into the evening, and when a lot of people are working remotely it can turn into a game of chicken (competition) over who logs off last.

Just don't play that game. You shouldn't feel you have to be constantly 'on', unless that's a feature of the job you've signed up to and you're being properly remunerated for it.

Hard at work or hardly working?

On the other hand, don't be tempted to go to the opposite extreme... Remote working operates on the basis of mutual trust. If you're never at your laptop when somebody happens to be looking for you, they might assume you're skiving. Most managers won't mind if you need to pop out during the daytime for a personal errand, like going to the dentist or picking up a prescription, provided you let them know what you're doing. Communication is key here.

Staying in touch doesn't mean you need to send your manager an hourly e-mail saying: 'I'm still working, not off down the pub'. Equally, your manager shouldn't be left feeling you've gone undercover (unless you actually do work for MI5[1]). It's more about letting them know in advance if you aren't going to be online for a while, and the reason for that. In summary, taking two minutes

---

1   The UK's security service. Top secret place doing top secret stuff.

to stick on a load of laundry is generally fine, but if you're going to be MIA (missing in action) for perhaps an hour or more you should make that known.

You should also check with your manager if you want to vary your daily work pattern. If you're a night owl, you might prefer to start and finish work late but that might not suit your colleagues.

If you manage staff, you should agree with them what work you expect them to get done by when and make an extra effort to stay in touch with them to see how they're getting on and deal with any queries.

Online meetings

A whole new etiquette has evolved around online meetings. Sigh. But some of it may work in your favour. Hurrah!

Setting up

When you're setting up for a virtual meeting, false onscreen backgrounds have proved popular in recent times. On the plus side, they can hide a multitude[2] if where you live isn't quite The Ritz.[3] Maybe we're just getting old and cranky (*speak for yourself – Debby*) but we're not big fans of them, since it can be quite distracting to other viewers if you look like you're being absorbed by a palm tree.

If you need to use one rather than sharing your unwashed crockery with the world, we recommend you avoid the 'busy' backgrounds and go for something plain.

---

2   Short for 'hide a multitude of sins' – meaning hide something you don't want others to see, like the mess in the room you're using for your virtual meeting.

3   Don't be thinking we mean Ritz crackers. We mean The Ritz as in the very posh luxury hotel in London.

A right dressing down

The dress code when you're attending a meeting from home tends to be a bit more fluid, which may mean you get to wear clothes you find more comfortable. Be prepared to see other people looking a bit different when they're working remotely too – it can be a shock to the system the first time you see the boss in a T-shirt and hoodie rather than a smart suit. If you're meeting with someone important, like a key client, you may still need to smarten up, though (at least from the waist up). As ever, you can take your cue from what your colleagues are doing.

Lights, camera, action!

It can be quite discombobulating to have to look at yourself on screen, unless you happen to resemble Chris Hemsworth[4] or Zendaya[5] (Debby didn't know who this was, but Maura assured her it's an actual celebrity, not a new fitness regime). It's generally expected you should keep your camera on; keeping it switched off during a meeting can be perceived as rude. Think of it from the perspective of the poor sod chairing the meeting – no mean feat if there's a screenful (or multiple screens) full of people and you're trying to work out who everybody is. They have no way of knowing whether you're paying attention or doing your Wordle.

However, if keeping your camera off really helps you to focus better, then go for it – but it's better to let someone know in advance since, as we said in Chapter 3, a simple explanation will work wonders.

Take a little time to set up your computer for online meetings so that you don't appear in half-darkness looking like you're about to conduct a séance. A screen light doesn't cost much and will

---

4   Popular Australian actor who, according to Maura (and quite a few million others), is handsome.
5   American actress so famous that she's only known by her first name. Except that Debby hadn't heard of her.

help you with this. Be ready for the meeting five or ten minutes in advance, having tested your sound, etc., so that you are nice and calm when it starts. You can always carry on working whilst you're waiting for the meeting to start. If there is a problem with sound, you can use the meeting's chat facility to communicate, as not everyone's a master of sign language.

If you log onto the Zoom today, you're sure of a big surprise...

Yes, some people use online meetings as their very own teddy bears' picnic. Maura recalls sitting through a meeting whilst the person chairing it grabbed a bite of lunch. In fairness, this hard-working soul had been taking back-to-back meetings all day without a break so was in dire need of sustenance, but Maura did find herself wishing they hadn't chosen soup for their midday repast. So much slurping...

If you must eat, and others on the meeting don't mind you doing so, at least put yourself on mute. Just remember to unmute when you need to speak – nobody wants to be the recipient of 'You're on mute!' if they can help it. If you're going to be called upon to address the meeting at any stage, it's best to wait until after you've spoken to start your lunch. Most people aren't well-versed in the art of sandwich crumb conversation. Plus, choking all over the computer is distinctly unprofessional and will alarm the cat, too, who failed to kill you earlier whilst attempting to be a trip hazard.

Having a quiet sip of water or a hot drink is generally considered okay, as long as you don't throw it over yourself whilst trying to focus on two things at once (Debby's trick) or gulp the end of it too loudly.

Pet peeves

The species most excited about the cultural shift towards home-working is the dog. Cats, not so much. We have no idea about snakes, iguanas and the like but we're pretty sure they'll have noticed the change, too.

If you have a dog, they will be absolutely thrilled you're spending more time with them and they will let you know this loudly and often. They will also assume this is the sole reason you're there and will be quite put out when they don't get to enjoy the level of attention from you they believe they deserve.

They will also let you know this loudly and often.

Cats may be indifferent (or even resentful) towards your extra presence but they don't half love a keyboard and online meetings may be fascinating – all those small on-screen creatures moving their heads like a mini aviary! Maura's cat fancies himself as a floof-reader and luxuriates across her desk at every opportunity. Debby's cat sees a pile of paperwork on the floor as an invitation to rip it to shreds, so if your cat also enjoys falling asleep on pristine forms you've just signed or worse, you might want to place up high anything you wish to keep intact.

Maura has a colleague who is genuinely terrified of animals so she shows them proper consideration when they're in a meeting together by keeping her pets well out of sight. However, most people don't mind if a furry friend pops up occasionally, and a well-timed cat posterior in the camera has been known to lighten the mood. However, if they end up being overly disruptive, you may have to give them a time out.

It's the same for clocks, we're afraid. Debby's family heirloom, a quirky grandmother clock, has a habit of bonging its head off during crucial moments of an interview. Whilst they can't always be shifted, you may have to stop that pendulum for the duration of the meeting.

CHAPTER 14

E-MAILS AND PHONE CALLS

It's amazing that more isn't written about e-mail, since we've known some people who are wonderfully warm in person, but judging from the tone of their e-mails you'd think they robbed the tooth fairy for fun.

Don't get us wrong, e-mails are great, because you get to tell people what you want without having the headache of an actual conversation.

However, the bad news is that you can't always get away with simply slinging a string of requests at someone without one word of type-written conversation.

So, if you're ready for some e-mail surgery, let's dissect the average e-mail bit by bit.

Great e-mail habits

1. The subject header
It really helps to type the point of the e-mail in the subject header, rather than 'Good morning' or something vague. If you're searching for this e-mail at a later date, you'll save yourself oodles of time. We don't know what an oodle of time is, but anyway you'll save it.

Because you've labelled the subject header, the other person will know roughly what your e-mail is about, so it also helps them to prioritize their list of e-mails waiting to be read. We're guessing that if you really want their attention quickly, you could put 'Arggghhhhhh!!' in the subject header, but it's probably not very appropriate unless there's a fire in the building.

2. Addressing a person

Is it 'Dear' like in a letter? Is it 'To' like on an envelope? Is it 'FAO' (for the attention of...) because you don't know exactly who to write to? Oh, boy.

If you know the person and want to address them informally, you can simply start the e-mail 'Hi Anita'.

In Maura's team, because they send each other so many e-mails they usually just start with the person's first name or initial.

If you know the person less well, we've found that the best e-mail etiquette is simply to write 'Good morning' 'Good afternoon' or 'Good evening' followed by the person's first name. And no, it doesn't matter if your time zone is different to theirs, don't worry about getting their time of day correct.

The best thing about e-mails is that when a person replies, they will sign the e-mail in the way they want to be addressed. You'll be forgiven for getting it wrong once as long as you take the hint by looking at their signature when they reply.

You know how you've had to get good at observing people and mirroring what they do over the years? Here's one of those areas where you can put those finely honed observational skills to good use – you can watch how your colleagues and contacts address their e-mails and respond in kind.

3. Greeting

If you're in a tearing hurry to get some work done, it's very easy to send an e-mail which is entirely demands, questions or both.

If this is the first time you've contacted the person about this issue, a quick first line to say you hope they're doing well today (or similar) softens the blow before you make any requests.

4. Content and tone

When you need someone to do something for you, try and avoid very stark e-mail demands.

Since you can't guess what kind of day the recipient is having, it's best to soften those requests in a way that won't make them feel tense.

Focus on asking them what they would be able to do, rather than what you need. For example, 'Would you be able to...?' generally sounds gentler than 'I need this by...' In effect, this shows the other person that you realize your requests aren't the only thing they'll have to deal with today.

You needn't shy away from the urgency of a request – you can certainly point out if you're working to a tight deadline, but just check with them whether what you're asking can be achieved.

5. Get to the point

People tend to get a lot of e-mails in an average working day and often scan them quickly first to see how much of their attention the message deserves. It's good, therefore, to let them know within the first few sentences (after your polite greeting) why you're contacting them and what you need them to do. If you don't need a response and are simply sharing information with them, you could start with 'This is just for your information...' or 'FYI' which stands for 'for your info', which I'm sure you'll be familiar with as you were paying attention in our abbreviations chapter.

E-mails should always be concise. If you need to provide a large amount of information, you would be better putting it into a Word document and e-mailing it over with a short covering message explaining what's inside.

6. Responding to e-mails

If you don't have enough information to answer an e-mail then and there, you might want to acknowledge that you've received the e-mail and say you're working on getting an answer to them. This prevents people from stressing that you didn't reply because you didn't get the e-mail.

7. Things to avoid in an e-mail

In an office e-mail, don't say anything about other people or yourself that you wouldn't want announced to the world in general. Apart from not being very professional, we're only too aware from personal experiences that one slip of the SEND button can mean that the wrong person is reading the essay on why your boss is a royal pain in the backside. By the wrong person, we generally mean your boss themselves.

If you want to get across the message that the tight deadline imposed on you has given you the urge to throw a custard pie in your boss's face, there are more subtle ways of saying so. Better to describe the situation rather than who's caused it.

'I've been given rather a tight deadline on this one' is preferable to 'that complete waste of space upstairs has asked for this within a week'.

8. Breathe before answering

Whilst it's good to get e-mails out of the way, we'd recommend that you don't reply to one immediately if it has made you feel angry. Flag it as new and leave it a while.

When we have been put in 'fight or flight' mode by an e-mail, our responses can be predictably sharp or defensive. Give yourself a little time to breathe, maybe squeeze something sensory and reply later when a two-worded curse isn't the first answer that leaps to mind.

9. Signing off

'Kind regards' tends to be the standard way of signing an e-mail these days. 'Best wishes' is also okay. Lazy so-and-sos sign off with the abbreviation for best wishes – 'BW'. They're obviously too important to type it out in full.

E-mails aren't formal letters, so if you have lots of qualifications you don't have to add them after your name unless you feel you'd like to make a point. Maybe leave out the cycling proficiency certificate, though.

10. Keeping tidy

We find the 'deal with it once' rule very helpful, if your role allows for this.

Lots of people open e-mails repeatedly throughout the day. E-mails are a great way to procrastinate, and they can be a phenomenal time-waster.

Only you can know how important it is that you check your inbox regularly for the role that you have. However, when you do read an e-mail, deal with it then and there whenever possible. If you can't reply to it when you've read it because you need more information (or you're picturing that custard pie again), you could flag it so it doesn't have to be searched for repeatedly among read e-mails.

Filing e-mails in online folders is a very handy way of not getting in an awful mess with a never-ending inbox of the darn things. If you've got a certain project on, it's a good idea to create an e-mail folder with the project title.

Be thorough about deleting any e-mails you don't need any more. It's the equivalent of keeping a tidy desk, and your brain will feel so much better as a result. If your organization has a policy on information management that requires you to maintain records, you might need to save some or all of your e-mails in a shared database before you delete them.

As with all tidying up, if you do a little every day, then you're not left with an unwieldy mess by the end of the month.

This also works for doing the dusting.

Great telephone habits

Unless you're chatting to a close colleague, phone calls have their challenges simply because they're auditory and often unexpected. The sound of a phone ringing may also startle you, annoy you by cutting across your thoughts or make you anxious.

If phone calls give you a headache, as we mentioned in Chapter 3, it's best to tell people that you prefer communicating by e-mail.

Equally, you might find a phone call preferable to a video call, and if you're just communicating with one person, they're unlikely to refuse you the right to communicate in the way that suits you best.

Some tips for phone calls:

Tip 1: Your voice

There are entire training courses dedicated to teaching people how to use an upbeat tone to send a virtual ray of sunshine down the phone. At the end of the day, if you're not that way inclined, by which we mean if you don't naturally sound like Mary Poppins,[1] you shouldn't have to fake it. It's nice just to greet someone by asking 'How are things with you?' at the start of a conversation. However, if you're speaking to the same person many times a day, you only need to bother the first time you chat to them.

---

1   Mary Poppins was known as a magical English children's nanny. She first featured in a series of books by P.L. Travers and was then the inspiration for a Disney musical film in the 1960s. It appears on British TV a lot.

Tip 2: Check in first

If you need to give a colleague a quick call, you don't need to pre-arrange to call them at a certain time. However, if you think you'll need to speak for longer than perhaps quarter of an hour, it's a good idea to ask them by e-mail or text if you can phone at a specific time when they're free to have a longer discussion.

Tip 3: Ask if they're free

If you're calling a colleague, just ask them quickly if they've got a moment to talk. A bit like when you've walked over to someone's desk, it's just a great idea to check that they haven't answered the call expecting it to be that urgent response they were waiting for from someone else. Or, they could be about to go into a meeting, or dying for a pee or something.

This is also a good tip for your home life. Just check when you call that it's convenient to chat otherwise you could be rushed to finish because someone else's oven chips are ready.

Tip 4: Orientate them

It's a great idea to fly a little verbal flag upfront to let the other person know what you're calling about.

'I've got a question about the document you sent over...'
'About the meeting that we've arranged for next week...'
'I just wanted to give you some feedback on the response I had...'

Whatever it is, wait a moment before dialling to think about that little summary line that will tell them what the call's about.

If you launch in too quickly, it's a bit like running round a track before the starting gun has fired. The other person is trying to play catch-up whilst their brain focuses on what exactly you're on about.

You might also find it helpful to jot down a few key points you wish to make before you pick up the phone, to help keep yourself on track. Speaking of which...

Tip 5: Keep a notepad ready

Keep a notepad handy so that you can write down anything important. Don't be shy about asking people to spell names or website addresses out, that's perfectly standard. If you missed something that wasn't quite clear, it's fine to ask: 'Sorry, could you say that again?' or 'I wasn't sure what you meant by...' You may be ultra-aware that your auditory processing isn't the same as others, but it's actually really good practice to ask for clarification and more people should do it. You can also test your understanding by saying 'Just to sum up what you've said...' and repeating back to them what your understanding of the situation is.

If something really is too complex for a phone call, ask them if they wouldn't mind summarizing what they've said in an e-mail.

CHAPTER 15

TAKING AND GIVING FEEDBACK

(or how to say 'that's rubbish' without getting sacked)

I n school, it's easy to know how you are doing; you get a grade, marks out of ten or a percentage. In the workplace, you're fortunate if your performance can be evaluated in terms of straightforward numbers. More often, you'll get verbal guidance on how you are doing, and you'll be asked your opinion on others' ideas, too.

Without receiving marks out of ten, things can get a bit vague and difficult to navigate. So, we've come to the rescue with a bit of guidance on what to expect.

Receiving feedback

It's common practice for employees to get regular feedback on their performance. Sometimes there's a formal process for this, such as an annual performance review, called an appraisal, where feedback is given to you both verbally and in writing.

Other than in your appraisal, feedback could be informal, like a quick 'catch-up' chat, especially if you're new to a role.

Getting feedback may seem daunting, but it's actually a good thing. It lets you know how you're doing at your job. A bit of positive feedback can improve your self-confidence. If the feedback shows there are skills or knowledge you need to develop further, it should be accompanied by suggestions for how you can do this – the offer of a training course or some online learning, perhaps. A good manager will always help their staff to give their best performance.

So, what should you do to prepare for your appraisal? Here are some tips:

Tip 1: Come prepared

Your manager may start off by asking you how *you* think you're getting on in the job, so you might want to have a think about that beforehand. It's a good technique, since it gives them a decent idea of how self-aware you are about your own strengths and weaknesses.

Tip 2: Ask for help if you need to

If there's something you feel you're struggling with, be honest about it and ask for suggestions on how you could improve and what support might be available. A feedback session is also a good chance to check in with your manager on how well (or otherwise) any reasonable adjustments are working and whether these need to be altered.

Tip 3: Try not to be overly defensive

It can be hard to take feedback that's not exactly glowing and your first instinct might be to defend yourself. If there's been some sort of misunderstanding or miscommunication, that's fair enough, but otherwise it's better just to listen and accept what's being said. If you don't know what to do about the feedback given, just ask them straight – how can I improve?

If you're unsure how to respond, you could say that you need to take time to reflect on what you've been told.

Tip 4: 'Room for improvement' doesn't mean you should quit

If you do receive feedback on where you can improve, please don't think that your boss is implying you aren't suited to the job, or should quit. New roles require a lot of getting used to and plenty of learning; no one expects perfection in the early months of a job.

We'd recommend that you give it at least six months in your new position before you decide whether or not you are comfortable in it. Be patient with yourself if you're not an expert at first. It wouldn't be a very rewarding role if you instantly grasped everything required.

Autistic people can be particularly harsh on themselves and expect too much too soon. If someone has taken the trouble to give you decent feedback, it means they feel you're capable of achieving better and they want to invest effort to make that happen.

Tip 5: Accept positive feedback

Weirdly, it can also be hard to take positive feedback, especially if you're autistic. What the heck are you supposed to say – 'Yeh, I am pretty amazing, aren't I?' would make you sound like a bit of a smug git, wouldn't it? Best to stick to a simple 'Thank you'. Plus, if you're not exactly brimming over with self-confidence and have grown up hearing all about your supposed 'deficits', being told something positive can create what's called cognitive dissonance – basically, your brain saying 'does not compute'.

TOP TIP: DON'T PUT YOURSELF DOWN

Maura was once offered the chance to pitch for a brilliant writing opportunity. It caught her by surprise so she panicked and spent the whole meeting enumerating the reasons why she probably wouldn't be any good at it. Don't do that.

Autistic people often thrive when allowed to play to their strengths – an approach that tends to be favoured in Eastern rather than

Western cultures, for some reason – and learning where those strengths lie could help you chart a more rewarding career.

Tip 6: Listen to all of the feedback

Managers often use what's known as a 'feedback sandwich'. There is no bread involved and no pickle on the side, sadly. It just means they'll say something positive about your work, mention something where there may be room for improvement, then finish on another positive. The idea is to avoid ending on a negative.

As soon as we hear anything negative said to us, though, we tend to fixate on that and zone out for the positives. It's a natural response and everybody does it. But if you perseverate on the Bad Thing, you won't properly absorb the positive feedback. Everyone has scope to learn, develop and grow. And that involves building on existing strengths as well as addressing any shortcomings.

Plus, understanding what you are doing well is really important, as you'll be more likely to repeat it.

Tip 7: Ask for directness

Although feedback that's a criticism can be hard to hear, what's even worse is when you're not entirely sure whether or not someone wishes to correct you. When people are trying to criticize in a kind way, they can be very vague, which doesn't always do autistic people any favours. From the outset, tell people that you appreciate it if they are direct and open with you, as you sometimes struggle to pick up hints. Just reassure them that they won't cause offence by communicating with you this way.

Giving your own feedback

One of the very best things about autistic people is that they tend to be honest and direct.

One of the main reasons autistic people get into bother is that they tend to be honest and direct.

As long as you're genuinely trying to be helpful, being frank about other people's ideas by using direct language is mostly very welcome. In fact, you may get a reputation for being the person that others go to if they want a straight answer without all the frills and fluff of non-autistic smooth-talking, conflict-ducking, polished-to-a-shine social niceties.

Telling it how it is – that's no bad thing.

However, a small word of warning. If your brain does happen to focus on detail, you can run the risk of always finding lots to criticize. We've known quite a few people who seem to find fault with everything; in fact their brains are in the habit of seeking it out as a kind of intellectual challenge. For the person you are talking to, listening to a list of things that are wrong can be quite draining if it happens all the time. Being presented with masses of problems can leave your listener with a mental burden.

This is why it's important to search for a balance when giving people feedback on their ideas. It might be worth pausing to think about how much the point you're thinking of making really matters. For instance, it bugs Maura when a questionnaire asks her whether she's 'neurodiverse' instead of 'neurodivergent' but whether she attempts to correct the person or organization asking depends on the context.

So, think about the *purpose* of the feedback you've been asked to give – and this will help you to decide whether or not to point something out.

So, let's assume your feedback is relevant. How can you express it in a really helpful way?

Please don't lose that awesome directness, but here is some guidance to ensure that you avoid getting dismissed as 'negative' or 'moany'. Yeh, you guessed it, more tips...

Tip 1: Give praise where it's due

Giving praise when you're in agreement or think something's good is a fantastic habit.

It means that when you do have to be critical, people will really listen up. Others tend to dismiss the views of people who *always* praise as insincere (*'they don't mean it, they just don't want to hurt anyone's feelings – everything can't be that good'*). On the other hand, people who *always* criticize can give the impression that they'll never be satisfied, no matter what. (*'Don't bother, they're just a negative person'.*)

Phrases such as 'I like that idea' or 'I hadn't thought of that, that's a great point' as people are sharing their thoughts are really positive and give a thoughtful contrast to those more critical reactions.

If you can, say what you like about an idea before sharing any misgivings about it. This shows that you are weighing things up carefully.

Tip 2: Think about how to express negative feedback

Imagine if you were the person on the receiving end of feedback – how would you feel if somebody told you straight out they thought your performance was rubbish? What would you even do with that? We're not suggesting you should lie, but that you might want to find a way to make the feedback feel more constructive to the other person.

A solid rule is to focus on what you'd like **more of**, rather than what you'd like **less of**. People learn very little from the word 'don't'. They learn plenty from the word 'do'.

For example, instead of telling somebody 'You talk too much' you might want to say 'I would like the opportunity to contribute more during our conversations'.

Here are some more examples of negative feedback, with more helpful ways of phrasing the same criticisms.

Negative feedback	More helpful way of putting it
Could you let me get a word in once in a while do you think, instead of gabbling at the speed of light?	I like it when you give me a little more time to digest what you're saying, as pausing really helps me to think.
You speak in jargon that I don't understand.	Keeping terminology simple helps me when you're talking, as I don't always understand the phrases you're used to.
You give me work without any thought to what I'm already doing.	It would be helpful if I could let you know what I'm already working on and the time that is expected to take, before I get given new tasks.
I give you a deadline and you never meet it, which slows me down.	Am I being realistic with deadlines? Is there any way we can make this easier for you to meet the ones I give?

Positive phrasing is particularly crucial for giving your manager '360 degree feedback'. That phrase is certainly a contender for the Beautiful Crap Award. It means your boss wants their employees' feedback on their own performance, as well as feedback from their manager and peers. Yup, your boss wants to hear if they're a good boss or not.

Bear in mind, you've still got to work with them the next day. So, come up with some positive ideas on improvements – and leave out phrases such as 'Why don't you ever make your own coffee, you lazy sod?'

Tip 3: Be balanced with the criticism

If there's something you're not happy about, it's tempting to focus on that thing. It's better if a complaint or concern is accompanied by some positive feedback. Remember the feedback sandwich? However, do ensure that the positive feedback relates to the same topic.

For instance, feedback such as 'You're really good at spreadsheets, pity you're rubbish at sending them to me on time. That's a nice stapler you've got there', is not going to work. Better to say something like: 'You're really good at spreadsheets, though it would be helpful if you could get them to me sooner. It's great you take such care with getting them right'.

Tip 4: Don't assume people know what they're doing well
Other people may not be as confident as they seem and may be delighted if you praise their performance.

Managers are the ones who most appreciate positive feedback, as it's often assumed that because of their leadership role, they don't need praise. Occasionally saying 'I really appreciate your support on that' or acknowledging the efforts that they go to in order to make life easier for their staff tends to be genuinely appreciated.

In general, showing appreciation for another person's efforts, even if it's part of their job, is a great idea and helps make relationships at work run smoothly.

Giving feedback takes practice and you will get better at it.

If you're still worried about it, you're welcome to practice on us by giving us feedback on this book.

Go on. We can take it...

CHAPTER 16

YOU WANT IT BY WHEN?!

Working to deadlines

Working in an office usually means having to plan ahead and multi-task. However, bear in mind that you don't have to be naturally good at everything, otherwise Maura would never ever have gone on a second date. Some of us are better at these things than others, autistic or not, but there are certain ways in which autism may create a few additional barriers.

We're also mindful that ADHD is a common 'co-star' of autism (here, we're grateful to Canadian advocate Jen Smits for coming up with such a brilliant alternative to the ghhhastly term 'co-morbidity'). ADHDers tend to have to work that bit harder again at planning and organization (though they usually excel at many other things, like staying focused in a crisis).

If you struggle with planning for deadlines, the first step is to identify what might be holding you back and the second is to figure out what you can do about it.

You probably have better analytical and problem-solving skills than a lot of people, and here is your chance to put them to good use.

What might be holding you back?

A lot of it comes down to a thing called 'executive functioning'.

This is a term given to the set of cognitive processes that allow us to manage our thoughts and actions. It's like having a supervisor in your head, complete with notepad and pen.

Executive functioning is what allows us to break a task down into steps and put them into the right sequence, another one of those things you're expected to have absorbed from the people around you from an early age.

> **Executive functioning:** The process by which the brain makes decisions through planning and organizing ideas and thoughts.

It sounds deceptively straightforward, doesn't it? But what if you can't work out what the first step is supposed to be? That's when 'task inertia' can kick in – when you struggle to get started on something. It can be mistaken for laziness, but it's so much more than 'not feeling it' or procrastination.

> **Task inertia:** When you find it hard to get started on something.

As a teenager (back when she had every intention of marrying George Michael), Maura used to freeze whenever her mother told her to 'Go clean the house'. What the heck did that mean? Where should she start? Her mother would inevitably find her an hour later still staring at a tin of furniture polish like it was an unexploded bomb.

The comforting bit

Yup, if you're autistic you'll no doubt find that your executive functioning skills aren't at the top of the leader board.

However, many non-autistics also lack executive functioning skills. There is a spectrum when it comes to executive functioning skills; some people score 10/10 and other people don't score highly at all. Autistic people don't tend to score highly at this (sniffle), but there are many non-autistics who also struggle when it comes to planning and organization skills.

You only have to observe the absolute mayhem in shopping centres on Christmas Eve (please don't, it's basically a horror movie designed for autistic people) to guess that last-minute shoppers can't all be autistic. They're simply people who either lack executive functioning skills, or used them all up on something else and had no brain power left for Christmas.

The advantage you have, courtesy of us (ahem), is that you're at least aware that your executive functioning skills may need a little toning up, and that's a pretty useful thing to know about yourself. Because now you can do something about it.

You're welcome.

It's not you, it's them...

If you find yourself with a huge list of things to do and at a loss as to where you should even start, it might not be purely because the executive functioning fairy was off partying with the social skills fairy on the day you were meant to be bestowed with her sacred knowledge.

In recent years, organizations in all sectors – public, private, voluntary and community – have been feeling the pinch (not literally) as a result of the overall economic situation. The trend has been for the size of many workforces to reduce, though the expectations and demands of service users and clients may have gone up.

So, there may be fewer people in a team doing the same amount of tasks as they used to do in a larger team. It may seem unfair that you're probably being expected to do more than someone in the same job ten years ago, but it's often the reality.

That may mean you have been given too much to do or unrealistic deadlines to do it in, and that you may be faced with too many competing demands whilst having the work of more than one person. Your workday may have more plot twists than *Game of Thrones*.[1]

What can you do about difficult deadlines?

The good news is, there's plenty you can do to help yourself if you get stuck. (We hesitate to call these 'life hacks' – we're really not that cool.)

Tip 1: Seek clarification

You may not need to complete every task that's been given to you immediately. When someone gives you a task, check out the deadline. Some are likely to be more important or more time sensitive than others, and it's perfectly reasonable to ask which one you should be tackling first and the relative priority of the others.

If you need to, you can ask for further clarity on what you're expected to do with a particular task. We don't recommend you saying: 'What the hell am I supposed to do with this?' Er, no. Better to say something like: 'This is what I'm minded to do but before I start I want to check I'm on the right track here'. It shows you're not expecting your manager to do all your thinking for you.

Tip 2: Asking 'Why?'

This is a very long tip and part way through it might escape your mind that Tip 3 is actually on its way soon, but it's very important and we ask for your permission to go on a bit...

If someone asks you to do something, it should be perfectly reasonable to ask them why they want you to do it, or why it has

---

1   Fantasy TV drama with 73 episodes. It follows a web of political conflicts among noble families and is the type of thing that requires a bit of concentration. If you brush the cat whilst watching you'll miss something critical (said from experience).

to be done a particular way, right? Well, yes and no. Sarcasm alert: That's helpful, isn't it?

After we'd written the first draft of this book, we asked some autistic employees to read it and let us know whether they found it useful. One of them shared with us that early on in their career they'd been accused of being defiant and not respecting a supervisor's authority, simply because they asked 'Why?' a lot. We thought it was a brilliant point so we added this section into the book.

Hence Tip 1 is asking for clarification and Tip 2 will tell you how to do it in a way that doesn't make you look like an awkward so-and-so.

When asking for clarification, if you just reply with 'Why?' the other person could perceive it as a challenge. It turns out that it's not *what* you ask, it's *the way* that you ask it.

Remember the problem we mentioned earlier in this book – you're expected to understand *them*, but they're not expected to understand *you*? This is a great example of how it can happen.

In non-autistic land, an abrupt 'Why?' is associated with being resistant to doing a task, like you're a teenager not wanting to tidy your bedroom. Similarly, if you ask a barrage of questions before agreeing to go off and do something, your colleague may think you're being negative by deliberately looking for problems.

In reality, you're probably just trying to understand the purpose of the request and the logic behind it, or wanting more clarity to ensure you deliver a good result. Some autistic people like to have as much detail as possible, since front-loading information gives them more certainty, and certainty is security.

Be aware, too, that anxiety can sometimes come across as irritability to someone else, depending on your facial expression or tone of voice, for instance, if you're frowning furiously trying to picture how this is going to work or just not sounding very positive.

A good manager should be willing to give you some context for a request, which is sometimes referred to as 'the big picture' (nothing to do with oversized artwork), and if you frame your question tactfully (again, no artwork involved), your queries will make you look thoughtful rather than belligerent.

So, instead of an abrupt 'Why?' how about saying something like: 'It would really help me to get a bit of context here, so I can understand what you need?'

The second approach is much softer. If you're stuck, think of it this way: you're telling them WHY you're asking WHY.

If you think a colleague hasn't approached something in the way that you would, instead of approaching them with 'Why have you done it like that?' a great alternative is 'Is there a reason why you've thought of doing it this way?' It took Debby roughly 35 years to work out that this phrase gave people enough space to justify their thinking and prevented her from assuming they'd miscalculated.

It could be the case, though, that you do have actual concerns about the request – for instance, whether it's the best approach to take or a good use of your time – especially if you suspect it hasn't been properly thought through.

Here, you need to tread carefully since if you point out to your superior (in rank, at least) that you think they're talking utter nonsense, it could end up being a career-defining moment, and not in a good way...

A better approach might be to say something like: 'Before I get started on that, I just want to settle my mind on some things if I may?' That way, you sound willing but have created an opening to draw out their thinking.

If you don't agree with their clarification, rather than saying: 'That won't work', you could try the less abrupt: 'I wonder if we've thought about/considered...?' This subtler technique stops people from being defensive and starts them on the process of problem-solving as a team.

And yes, we get it. You really mean 'I wonder if *you'd* thought about...' Using the word 'we' distances you from criticizing someone else directly; this problem belongs to *us* as a team, no matter who thought of it as an obstacle. You'd be amazed at how well people respond to that.

Be prepared for some of your questions to be met with: 'Don't worry about that yet', or 'Let's cross that bridge when we come to it' (which means 'We'll think about that later'). What the other person is implying here is: 'I think that's a minor detail and it's unimportant to me at this stage, so it should be to you as well'. They may have a point; it could genuinely be too soon to know the answer. Trying to pin down too much of the detail or look too far ahead may well be draining for both of you if it's not really necessary. Sometimes conscientiousness can tip over into perfectionism.

Alternatively, their reticence to answer your queries might be caused by a realization that they do need to put some more thought into this – only they don't want to admit it.

Either way, they're signalling to you that they won't welcome further questions at this stage. In that case, it's best to accept you need to go ahead with the information you have available to you.

If you come across a lot of minor queries whilst you're doing a piece of work and don't want to keep interrupting someone, it can be a good idea to write a list of questions and e-mail them over. You can start the e-mail with something positive, such as 'I'm making some progress with this and just have a few queries for you before I continue...' It's unlikely someone would argue with that one.

Now, without further ado, let's move onto the next (far shorter) tip.

What do you mean, '*Why?*'

Tip 3: Negotiate

If a deadline feels too tight, there may be scope to ask for an extension of time. Sometimes a manager will give you a deadline, but really they've built in some extra time and it isn't as strict as it looks. Perhaps they've done this to give themselves time to review what you produce, or to allow for other delays. Either way, you can ask if there is any flexibility on a deadline that seems like a tough one to meet.

Tip 4: It doesn't have to be right first time

Procrastination and perfectionism tend to go together. When you feel you have to get something perfect first time, it can make a task too daunting. Many autistic people are very thorough and attentive to detail, and the concept of doing a rough version of anything feels a bit beneath them.

Take a deep breath. Most work goes through development stages before it's fine-tuned, and it's far easier to refine a piece of work than to start it from the beginning.

TOP TIP: DON'T BE PUT OFF BY DEADLINES
Start small and simple, and build on it.

Tip 5: Make a deadline chart

It might be helpful to take a look at when your task has to be done by and work out how many working days you have left until the deadline.

You could make this into your very own chart. It's handy if you can use a wipe-clean board so that you can count down the number of days left on your chart daily and see which tasks are more urgent at a glance.

Tip 6: Timings

Tasks that take under an hour to complete aren't usually that daunting. Tasks that take over an hour and much focus (like a report) are more likely to be daunting; they tend to get put off.

In office-speak, doing loads of reactive stuff at the expense of larger, more strategic tasks is known as 'fire-fighting'.

The answer is to break down tasks that are over an hour into smaller ones you can more easily tackle.

For instance, for a report, you might want just to put 'Report introduction' on your to-do list.

Creating a series of smaller tasks will make you better organized and far less likely to put off important jobs.

Tip 7: Set reminders

If you have competing demands, you could put reminders for when certain tasks are due to be completed into your work calendar or onto your phone, if that works for you.

Visual reminders are always helpful, so you could keep a monthly calendar which has a generous space for each day, so that you can 'see' the time ahead and note anything important on it. Week view diaries can also be helpful if you need to block out time for tasks on one particular day. Some people, however, are very adapted to working with phone apps that they find just as helpful. Whatever works!

Tip 8: Use routine to your advantage

It bugs both of us that a need for routine is so often considered a 'deficit' among neurodivergent people.

Sure, if routines become so rigid that they prevent you doing other things, they may tip into that, but most of the time they can be really useful.

Sometimes we just fall into a routine naturally but other times we can create them by thinking about the steps involved and then repeating them.

If you establish an order for doing things in, this may help you ensure they get done in a way that requires minimal thought. For instance, having a morning routine for self-care means you don't have to think about whether to brush your teeth before you shower or vice versa – you can just get on with it without draining your mental battery by having to work out what to do.

Similarly, in work, it may help to have a routine to start your day – checking your unread e-mails, making a list of the tasks for the day, etc.

Part of your routine could be to plan ahead for the next day. This may include figuring out what you're going to wear rather than staring unblinkingly at your wardrobe the next morning before your first caffeine fix as though you're waiting for a character from Narnia[2] to tell you which trousers to put on.

One less thing to think about leaves you with more mental energy for the day ahead.

Tip 9: Discuss unrealistic deadlines

If you find that you are stressing out about deadlines, ask yourself one question: 'Given the task ahead and the deadline, could *anyone* be realistically expected to complete it in time?'

Often we blame ourselves for not working fast enough. If you take a step back and look at the situation, you might come to the conclusion that even the fastest, most competent worker could not be expected to achieve what you've been set in the time given. It might simply be too much for one person.

It could be that the people around you don't understand the full complexity of a task, or they don't appreciate the other jobs you're also trying to complete within a narrow timescale. Pessimistically, it could be that they recognize the stress you're under but it's become part of the office culture.

Before you chat to a manager about the deadline, ask yourself a few questions:

---

2   Narnia is the fantasy world from C.S. Lewis's 1950 fictional tale *The Lion, The Witch and the Wardrobe*.

- Are there any parts of this project that could easily be given to someone else?

- Are you expecting too much of yourself? Autistic people are often attentive to detail and can be perfectionists. So check with others in the team that your standards aren't so high that they are making a deadline out of reach. If they do need to be this high, then it's the deadline that will have to be moved.

- If you have to have a deadline discussion, it's better to ask for a private chat. Point out what can be achieved within the deadline and what can't. If you have more than one task to be completed within a narrow timeframe, and you're not sure where to focus your energy, ask them which should take priority.

Tip 10: Focus on what you can do, not what you can't

It's a grown-up, confident thing to do, to have that tricky discussion with a manager. We promise, though, that it's always good for a boss to get warning that a deadline can't be met, rather than finding out at the point where nothing can be done. They would also rather you told them that your resources were stretched than lose a great member of staff through stress.

What managers really don't appreciate is people who constantly moan at them without giving any solutions. When they use the yuck beautiful crap 'be solution-focused' they really mean 'quit moaning and giving me obstacles'. Ready for our old friend the golden nugget of positive phrasing?

If you're having difficulty and it's going to be bad news for them, you might want to have an alternative plan or solution ready to discuss. For instance, how much longer do you need to complete the project? Would this reduce if someone else took one other task from you? What kind of detail or quality would need to be dropped in order to meet the deadline?

In summary, then, we suggest you:

1. Make yourself a chart with deadlines on it, so that you can see clearly how long you have left for each job.
2. Before you add any large tasks, break them down into smaller chunks.
3. Then add those chunks to your to-do list.
4. If you can't make a deadline, approach your manager when you realize, tell them what's getting in the way, and suggest a solution.

A little secret: At first, Debby and Maura both found that competing demands meant that writing this book, a project that at first was without any deadline, stayed at the bottom of the to-do list. However, we both set aside a small amount of time, half an hour a day, to at least get started. As writers, we know that you can spend quite a long time staring at a page. But give it half an hour a day and suddenly you've got something to share. Between us, we conjured up enough work to become enthusiastic and then completing it became easier. It was getting started that was the hard bit.

CHAPTER 17

LOOKING AFTER YOURSELF

We all have good days and bad days. On the not-so-good days, there may be things you can do to improve your mood. Even better, if you can figure out what things drain or overwhelm you, and what helps restore you, you can dodge your stressors and triggers when that's possible or at least have a plan in place for when they're unavoidable.

What to do when you're feeling a bit rubbish

Listen to your own body

Sometimes, when you're autistic, you might not immediately know why it is you feel out of sorts. There's this thing called 'interoception', which is the ability to pinpoint how you're feeling (not to be confused with the movie *Inception*,[1] which is only mildly more confusing). Autism seems to mess with that a bit.

That's why it's important to 'check in' with your body on a regular basis. Are you angry or just hungry? ('Don't make me hangry,

---

1   *Inception* (2010) is a mind-bending futuristic film starring Leonardo DiCaprio and directed by Christopher Nolan.

you wouldn't like me when I'm hangry', as an autistic Hulk[2] might say.) When's the last time you had a glass of water? Do you need to pee? It's easy to ignore the signals your body is trying to send you when you're completely engrossed in something, but you'll feel much better if you take that loo break or refuel when you need to.

If you reach for a packet of crisps instead of having a proper meal, it might be because you've waited until you're ready to chew your own arm off (figuratively speaking) instead of planning to eat at a sensible time.

Adjust your environment

Remember how we talked about identifying and avoiding sensory stressors in Chapter 3? Even when those of us who are sensory defensive have explained that fluorescent lights and competing noises are a recipe for misery, and a probable migraine, other people just tend to forget because they're not experiencing those things in the same way.

Office workers tend to snap on overhead lights as soon as they walk into a room without thinking about it, for instance. Whilst it can feel like a real pain to have to ask constantly for your reasonable needs to be met, better to do so (politely) than to sit there and suck it up all day. Or if some people really do need the extra light, you could suggest turning some of the lights off or letting you do your work somewhere else.

Something to watch out for is that sensory aversions can be dynamic – that is, there are likely to be times when sensory input is harder for you to process, like when you're tired.

Another one to be alert to is that autistic people tend to soak up bad vibes in a room and absorb other people's stress. When

---

2   The Incredible Hulk is a Marvel Comic superhero known for getting very big, strong and green when angry. Inconvenient if you're due to visit the mother-in-law.

you were a kid at school, and another kid was being told off by a teacher, did you feel as though you were the one in trouble? Don't get us started on the autistics lacking empathy myth (again).

Both of us have had the unfortunate experience of working in a toxic work environment. If you find yourself in one, as far as possible stay out of office dramas and avoid the individuals who seem to feed off them. Don't fight other people's battles for them and don't take on responsibility for solving other people's problems, especially if you're in an office with more drama than an *EastEnders*[3] Christmas special.

Practice self-care

Many years ago, long before she had any inkling she was autistic, Maura's yoga teacher told her she had the stiffest shoulders she'd ever seen (most probably because that's where Maura carries the weight of the world). Shortly after that she won a voucher for a free massage, so our intrepid author decided to give it a go. Only it turned out to be one of the worst experiences of her life. All that... touching.

The point here – yes, this story does have an actual point to it – is that self-care is not the same for everyone. So if scented candles make you gag or the only thing you get from a long soak in a bubble bath is wrinkly fingertips, don't worry about it. You do you.

At the risk of sounding like a 1950s public health infomercial, fresh air and exercise usually do help. Natural light and spending time in nature work well for some people as well.

And then there's whatever your intense interest or passion is – the thing that gets you into a flow state and makes time vanish whilst you're enjoying it.

---

3   British soap opera that's been running since 1985 and is known for saving up its most dramatic storylines for the Christmas Day special, so that we all have problems digesting our dinner.

Certain routines or rituals can be soothing, too – in other words, the very things that are usually described in textbooks as 'deficits' may well be your best coping mechanisms.

Avoid developing unhealthy coping mechanisms, though – alcohol or junk food might give you a temporary boost and are okay in moderation but if you find yourself becoming overly reliant on them, take stock and think about what you can do instead that's better for your health longer-term.

Respect your limits

If your workload is stressing you out, maybe you're setting overly high expectations for yourself. Perfectionism is common among autistics, along with conscientiousness and an imagination so strong it can result in catastrophizing: in other words, the key ingredients for stress.

When you're in that state, there's a temptation to think the only way to keep on top of things is 'if I just work harder' or 'if I keep going for longer'. But work is a marathon, not a sprint, and there are extremely few jobs that are worth risking complete burnout. Is anybody going to die if you leave that spreadsheet until the morning? The likelihood is you'll do a better job of it if you come into work the next day refreshed.

If you find you tend to put too much pressure on yourself, remember the value of a human being does not depend on their productivity. You deserve rest and recreation without having to 'earn it'.

You are good enough.

Stand up for yourself

If you feel you're being unfairly treated, or think someone is being deliberately nasty to you, it's a good idea to talk it through with a trusted friend or colleague.

Like we said in Chapter 10, it's best to try to resolve workplace problems informally at an early stage, since formal procedures for dealing with them can be stressful in themselves and create additional conflict. You can also use the advice in Chapter 15 on giving feedback to help tackle problems early.

Don't suffer in silence, and make sure you have someone to support you.

When it goes horribly wrong...

Okay, so you've made a mistake. Or something hasn't gone your way at work and it's ended up in a result that is disappointing or making you anxious.

Unfortunately, being autistic, you most probably have a more sensitive emotional alarm system than a lot of people. Your inner Health and Safety Executive (we all have one, it's called a survival mechanism) slams on the 'red alert' button quite enthusiastically at the first sign of trouble and shouts 'EVACUATE THE BUILDING!!'

Except you can't do that, because you're at work.

In terms of the main survival responses, *fight*, *flight* or *freeze*, your brain is so darn busy trying to avoid you running out the office screaming (*flight*), that your highly alert nervous system is forced into *freeze* mode instead. Mostly because the other ancient survival option, *fight*, is distinctly inappropriate at work.

Now, freeze mode was possibly helpful over a few thousand years back, when you didn't want a charging bison to notice you. Blending in with the background – great.

Unfortunately, we have the same kind of lower brains that we did back then, which is a bit of a shame as this mode is distinctly unhelpful in an office crisis.

So, how do you shift out of 'freeze' mode?

First steps

The first thing we'd like you to do is to recognize your emotional state.

Check in with your body, be aware that because of what's happened, you are tensing up, your heart is quickening and your thoughts are rushing. You can't get out of freeze mode if you're not aware you're in it.

Second, take a breather. Literally. Step away from your desk and go somewhere quiet to do some slow breathing. If you can, walk around a bit, preferably outdoors. Congratulate yourself. You're dealing with it. Give yourself 15 minutes if you can afford it just to slow down.

If your thoughts start to speed up again, watch them like an observer. Catastrophic predictions are just 'panic thoughts'. Label them as such. *'This is just my body telling me something has gone wrong'.*

Whatever you've done, no one has actually died (unless you're a heart surgeon, which is a different book entirely).

Remember also that even if you're not sure what to do, that doesn't mean there isn't a satisfactory resolution to the problem. It's just that you may not have enough information right now to deal with the problem.

It's important not to act straight away unless your mistake has led to an imminently catastrophic situation (see earlier mentioned book on heart surgery). Once your breathing and thinking has slowed, and you are out of freeze mode, you can move more steadily from crisis to action plan. Think of this as just a problem to be solved, like any other.

If it helps, think of yourself in the third person. *'This has happened. What is Maura going to do now?'* Or *'What will Debby do to rectify the situation?'*

Things go wrong at work. People make mistakes. Don't tell yourself you're a disaster just because you're a perfectionist and today you were human. It's okay.

If you were to remain in freeze mode, you'd do nothing, or cover your mistake hoping that no one would find out about it. This is a bad idea.

Honesty is the best policy, as soon as possible, so that there's a chance to put things right.

Tell someone

If you've messed up, or misunderstood something and you need a bit of help with it, tell someone as soon as possible. Usually, that will be your direct manager but if that's not a good option for any reason, at least immediately, tell someone who you trust, who is calm and collected. Not someone who will gasp and panic and make your anxiety a whole load worse.

Come up with options

You may not have the result you want, but once calm you may be able to think of a few options about what to do next. Sometimes, it really helps to give a boss bad news paired with some solutions.

> 'Okay boss, this has happened (describe the not ideal situation). So, I've thought about it and we can either now do this or this. Which approach would you favour?'

Accept responsibility

If you messed up or you could have handled things better, say so and apologize for any hassle you've caused. There may have been contributing factors, which you can mention, but if you sound as though you're trying to push the blame onto someone else you'll come across as defensive, at best.

Reflect later

Once you've got yourself an action plan and have moved on from it, find some quiet time at home to reflect. Why did things go wrong?

Sometimes it's because:

- we had too much pride to say we didn't know, so we guessed

- we rushed something and made a mistake

- we had a key piece of information missing and made a false assumption as a result

- we didn't have the skill to carry out a task

- we didn't ask for help when we should have

- we didn't give enough information about a task to someone else.

Do you need more coaching and training? Do you need to trust others around you more? Or drop your pride a little? Was it simply that you didn't ask enough questions first? (We know, we know, too many darn questions.)

Making mistakes is part of life. The most successful people use their mistakes as a learning tool. Reflection is a part of that process. You'll be extremely impressive in your annual review if you can demonstrate how you used a mistake to improve your own performance. Managers love that kind of stuff.

Fall down, then get back up. It's not because you're rubbish at your job. It's because you're getting better at it all the time.

Try to keep what's happened in perspective. In five years' time, will anyone ever remember this happened? Maura's mum has a favourite saying, 'This wee time will pass'. And it always does, no matter how bad it feels when you're in the midst of the problem.

Note: You're highly unlikely to be sacked
Young employees who are new to office life sometimes fear that if they make mistakes they'll be assumed incompetent and sacked.

So you'll probably appreciate knowing that actually, you can't be sacked that easily.

It's only if you do something horrendously wrong, and we're not talking making a small mistake here, that you can be dismissed immediately, which is called 'summary dismissal'. 'Summary' means immediate in this context and is usually on the grounds of what's usually referred to as 'gross misconduct'. This is rare. It would happen, for instance, if you were deliberately dishonest about something really important, did something dangerous or gave away company secrets. There are red lines (limits) not to be stepped over in any organization, and their conduct policies will tell you what those are.

When people are performing badly because they can't be bothered or are just shoddy in their work, an organization is generally obliged to give warnings – usually an informal warning first – and be clear about improvements that are needed before further disciplinary action, including dismissal, can take place.

In most sectors, people who make honest mistakes because they are learning would simply get more training and coaching, or perhaps their work would be monitored a little more closely.

So breathe, step away from panic thoughts, make yourself an action plan of what you're going to do next, and tell someone. It rarely is the end of the world, even if your slip-up is inconvenient or slows up progress a bit.

We've all made mistakes at work. You may feel that because you're autistic, you're the only one making them. But you're not.

Take it from us.

Spotting when someone's taking advantage

Looking after yourself at work means knowing when someone is asking too much of you.

This isn't necessarily personal; if you're obliging, hard-working and diligent, the chances are that sooner or later, someone may try and take advantage of this. It's not always that easy to spot when people are making you work harder than you should be.

Don't be persuaded to do something that is way outside of your comfort zone or puts too much stress on you, just because someone else can't be bothered to do that job.

How do you spot someone taking advantage of your diligent nature? Here's some things you may want to watch out for:

1. They suddenly want to be your best mate

Usually, this colleague can barely be bothered to say 'hi'. But for some reason, they've started complimenting you on your talents and skills. Alert! They could be inching towards the moment when they ask you for a favour. And because they've been so *nice* to you, you'll want to please them.

As long as it's okay with you and you don't mind doing a task, it's fine to help people out at work, particularly if you have expert knowledge which they lack.

Like any relationship, though, make sure that they put in as much effort as they get from you.

Read that again, it's really important.

Actually, we'll put it in a box. That's how important it is.

TOP TIP: DON'T FEEL YOU HAVE TO DO SOMEONE A FAVOUR

Before you do a favour, ask yourself whether this person ever does much in return.

Is this person friendly and do they treat you as a valuable colleague, or are they only pally when they want something from you?

Do they constantly ask you to do things for them, and you barely get a thanks?

If they're a supportive colleague and would help you in return, by all means help them out if you can.

However, if someone is not generally a supportive colleague and is constantly putting extra work on you, be brave. Put your own work first and say: 'I'm happy to do that for you, but it will have to wait until this is done'. Or, if it puts you under a lot of stress, just say: 'I'd love to help but I've really got too much on at the moment'.

You may worry that by saying 'No' you won't be liked, but if you say it pleasantly and politely, all that will happen is that people will develop a healthy respect for your boundaries.

In other words, they'll stop taking the piss (taking advantage).

This is a good thing. And it's taken both of your authors a long time to learn it...

2. They volunteer you for work without your permission

Unless they are your manager, it is not okay for someone to volunteer you for a job that's not yours, particularly in a meeting, without asking you first if it's okay by you.

It's one thing suggesting: 'George, I thought you'd be a good one for this – what do you think?' and quite another to assume you'll do it by saying: 'Right, we'll put George on that'.

The exception to this is a task that falls directly in your own area of expertise and no one else's.

For instance, if George is the IT specialist and the system has a hiccup, saying 'Right, we'll put George on that', is perfectly reasonable.

However, if it's a job that *anyone* in the team could do, and suddenly you find your name being put forward regularly, someone could be taking advantage of your willingness to please.

Now, let's not make hassle for the sake of it. If your name is put forward and actually it's for something that's entirely fine by you, you needn't say anything. But if you find yourself thinking 'Hold on, I didn't ask for that job nor do I want it...' it's worth pointing it out politely.

You don't have to have a confrontation in public, but how about in private pointing out your own situation? Something like: 'Before we commit to my name being down for that one, can we have a separate discussion about it? I've got quite a bit on'.

Through these words you're politely giving this unspoken message: 'I'm a willing worker but I'm not letting people take advantage of me'.

Mostly you only have to do this a few times before people learn to treat you with a little more respect.

If you always do whatever people ask, however inconvenient it is to you personally, you are training people to ask for whatever they want, whenever they want it.

Don't be unwilling or unhelpful. Just make sure you're not the only one saying 'yes' all of the time, when others are quite comfortably saying 'no'.

3. They don't put in their share of effort

If you are one of the many autistic folks out there who rise to the challenge of a deadline and work very hard to achieve it, you may be frustrated by those who don't do the same and let you down.

Be clear, through an e-mail if you like, what you need from them in order to proceed with your own work, and by when. A friendly way of doing this is to start the message with:

'Just a quick reminder...'

'Hope you don't mind a quick nudge, but I could do with...'

If the other person is dragging their heels (being slow) to the point where it's impacting on you, you can privately mention what you're waiting for, without judgement.

For instance, Maura could say to our publisher: 'I'm ready to send Chapter 4 through but I'm just waiting for Debby's corrections'.

If you're pretty certain that no one is getting into real trouble, it's okay to do that.

And if there's a hold up because of someone else and you really aren't sure what to do, have a quiet chat with your manager or a colleague you really trust. Maura calls people like these her 'wing mirrors' because they may see things she's missed.

> ## TOP TIP: GET A SECOND (OR THIRD) OPINION
> If you suspect someone is taking advantage, it's worth getting another perspective on the situation. Most people chat about their work to trusted friends and relatives. Describe the situation and get advice on what they think you should do.

Suspicious phrases

We don't want you to be suspicious of every colleague. However, if your instinct tells you that someone is being nice to you but you don't completely trust their motives, the chances are you are right. Sometimes you just can't interpret those instincts, to the point where you have an uneasy feeling but you don't quite know why.

Phrases like these can be a bit of a giveaway:

- 'This will be an excellent development opportunity for you'. Really? Will it? Or is it a job designed for someone above your pay level, that you will end up doing for less money? If you're not sure, say you'd like some time to think about it, and chat to family and friends before committing.

- 'This will raise your profile within the company'. The promise of kudos and a fab reputation shouldn't make you do something that's a rubbish task that you don't want to do at all. Again, think about the task and ignore the fluffy advertising speak that introduces it!

- 'You're really good at this, could you…?' can sometimes be translated as 'I don't want to do this, but if I shove a compliment your way, you might'. You might not mind, but if you do mind, point out that you have other priorities you have to finish.

Listen to your instincts, and be true to yourself and your own well-being.

CHAPTER 18

IT'LL BE FUN!

Christmas, the office social and other things you'd rather avoid

T here it is again, the S-word. You may be weary of how pre-occupied non-autistic people can be about how 'social' or otherwise you are. Many people seem to equate being 'sociable' with being 'nice', or to assume you can't possibly be enjoying life without a busy social calendar. (Somebody should really tell them about intense interests.)

Part of the problem is that, for many years, autism was framed almost exclusively in terms of social deficits. Things are starting to change, thankfully, but the general public still tend to think autism is solely about social awkwardness and that the solution is for autistics to be coached to be more socially competent, even if that's something that is waaaaay down their own list of priorities. We don't all want to be a social butterfly, Jemima.

Of course, it's perfectly possible you may enjoy socializing. Most autistics do to some extent, in the right circumstances: in the right environment, with the right people, for the right amount of time. Right on. Some autistics are even extraverts (how did that happen?). When you've met one autistic person, you've met one autistic person and all that. You do you – no judgement here.

Either way, though, office social events have a whole other set of unwritten rules and expectations. These unwritten rules are like the unexploded mines of the workplace – you've no idea they're there until you step on one. This chapter is about helping you avoid them.

What should you expect?

There are lots of different types of social gatherings associated with work. The bad news is that there tend to be differing expectations for each.

Some are mercifully short and relatively straightforward – meeting up for a slice of cake in the conference room on Sandra's birthday, for instance. Even if you're not the social type, you can probably join in with that in the interests of office harmony and politely excuse yourself after you've hung around long enough to pass yourself. How long that is may vary. In this example, 10 or 15 minutes ought to do it – and, really, nobody is going to be timing you with a stopwatch.

If it's an occasion where speeches are to be given, like a retirement party, it's polite to stay until after the formalities (speeches and gift-giving) are over. You can always arrive a bit later than the start time – speeches don't usually happen right at the start of proceedings.

It starts to get a bit more complicated when the social event is not being held in the office. It could be a really informal thing, like people casually meeting up for a quick pint on a Friday after quitting time. There's no real pressure for you to attend, but it might be a good way to get to know a few people better in more relaxed circumstances. You can always make some discreet enquiries about who's likely to be there to help you decide.

Or, it could be a more formal event, like a dinner for someone who's leaving the organization. In that case, you'll be expected to RSVP (repondez s'il vous plaît – why is it French? We don't know) and, if you're not planning on going, to say why – more about that below.

You should be aware that whether a social event is being held in the office or not, it's likely your office code of conduct will still apply, so we recommend you continue to follow our earlier advice about sticking to safe topics of conversation.

How much does it really matter?

Most people should be fine with you limiting or avoiding participation in social gatherings if they have some idea why you need to do that. The first time Maura decided to opt out of the office Christmas party, she was worried her colleagues might be offended but they were totally fine with it once she'd explained that noisy parties were less fun for her than root canal.

The exception here is entertaining clients (shudder). The non-autistic world seems to feel that business is done better between people who get on well. Paid for lunches can be a bit cringe (awkward); you might want to refer to our section on small talk if you need to survive one.

If you're in a team and you have a colleague who actually enjoys that type of stuff – hurrah! Nominate them for the lunch every time if you can get away with it.

'Working lunch' or just 'lunch'?

There's a difference between a 'working lunch' and just 'lunch'.

A 'working lunch' means having food, usually sandwiches, whilst you have a meeting together, which is perfectly acceptable to most people as long as the sandwiches are nice. However, if you have sensory sensitivities around the smell of some foods, this might feel like rather a trial. If so, you should definitely point it out beforehand rather than suffer in silence. It's not that people intend to be thoughtless or non-inclusive; this stuff just doesn't occur to them. And if your organization is forward-thinking, it could do everyone a great favour by engaging the services of someone like The Girl with the Curly Hair (aka Alis Rowe – see the support section at the end of the book) who offers terrific training on sensory matters.

When lunch is just a lunch out, as opposed to a working lunch, have a think about your options. If choosing from a menu at a restaurant is a nightmare for you, you have two choices. First, be honest, say that autism makes this kind of thing tough and you appreciate the offer but will politely have to decline.

Or second, suggest a place near to the office that you personally know well and are comfortable with. Once you're already accustomed to the menu and the atmosphere, the small talk is a little easier. Most restaurants have copies of their menus online as well, if you want to have a look at it in advance.

But hey, don't sweat it (worry). If these people knew what a burden their offers were, they wouldn't do it to you, honestly.

Christmas events

There's a reason these get their very own heading: *'tis the season to take cover, fa-la-la-la-laaa-la-la-la-la!*

When it comes to increased social demands, Christmas is the gift that keeps on giving, that gift often being a thumping headache from loud parties, tacky decorations and overpriced mass-produced meals. It can also be hugely irritating if you just want to get on with doing your work but other people are in 'Christmas mode' – they're all 'ho ho ho!' whilst you're 'no no no!'

You may arrive in the office one day to find there's been a tinsel explosion AND THERE'S NOT EVEN A 'D' IN THE MONTH. Take a deep breath. Aside from your own workspace, there's probably not much you can do about it, unless office decor falls within the scope of any reasonable adjustments you have in place.

If you aren't Christian, you may find all the festive fuss a bit of an affront. Similarly, if you are a religious Christian, you may also find the superficial spangly atmosphere a little unpalatable. This is because, as we're sure you'll have guessed, most office folk just use Christmas as an excuse to break up the daily monotony and do less work (not that useful if predictable routine works well for you).

One thing's for sure, saying 'I'm an atheist/agnostic/Jedi' when asked to help with the office decorations is a sure-fire way of being labelled a party pooper. It's not really about religion, it's about festive camaraderie, so don't feel you're 'selling out' if you embrace the atmosphere. Don't feel guilty about working a little less in December, either. It's almost guaranteed that office productivity falls off as people debate what they're going to wear to the Christmas do. Much as you might be focusing on your work, brace yourself for the fact that others may be in more of a 'tra la la' state.

'Secret Santa' is another tradition in some offices you may have to endure. If you don't, you may be regarded as a bad sport. You may have had to do Secret Santa at school, in which case you'll know how awkward it can be trying to buy a cheap gift for someone you hardly know.

Probably best to stick to a safe bet – bath foam or chocolate – rather than being too clever. Only buy someone a humorous gift if you're absolutely certain they'll appreciate it, since humour can backfire spectacularly if it's taken the wrong way.

There are some things you can pass on if you prefer, though, such as Christmas lunches or dinners. If you have staff, they might actually prefer you to give them some money for the drinks kitty and let them get on with it. Again, you can ask about what's involved before you decide.

Tips on social events

Tip 1: Weigh it up before you decide
Your instinctive reaction to a social invitation might be to avoid

it, or you might quite like the idea but get more anxious about it as it gets closer. But bear in mind that few decisions in life are irreversible and, worst case scenario, if you're having a miserable time you can always leave early. Plus, it's possible you might have a good time and develop your relationship with some of your co-workers. Social events are bonding experiences and you may feel like you've missed out if you're not part of them. As mentioned earlier, gleaning as much information in advance as possible (like who's going, when, where and for how long) can help you to make a properly informed decision.

Tip 2: Choosing what to wear
You could ask other people to help you decide what to wear for an event. In the fantastic short film *Mildly Different* (Czarska, 2021), our office hero misunderstands the dress code and arrives to a social do completely overdressed, which makes an awkward situation even worse. Similarly, being too casual for a posh event can make it look as if you weren't bothered to make an effort. If you find yourself asking lots of questions beforehand, you could explain that social dos make you rather anxious. For the record, 'black tie' means either a dinner suit or a dress – basically, the poshest outfit in your wardrobe. 'Smart casual' as we mentioned earlier in the book generally means to avoid jeans and trainers.

Tip 3: Planning your exit strategy
If you do decide to give a social event a try, having a plan for how and when you can leave may make you less anxious about it. There's nothing worse than worrying about how you're going to make your way home at chucking out (closing) time, especially if you're not sure when that might be. So, arrange a lift, book a taxi or check the availability of public transport.

Excuse yourself when you're ready to leave. Ducking out of a social event without saying farewell is considered bad form. It's sometimes referred to as an 'Irish goodbye', which is ironic since most Irish people we know tend to continue chatting for up to another hour after announcing they're leaving...

Tip 4: The hybrid solution – Drinks without a meal

Want to show willing but not commit to a full evening? As far as your escape route goes, drinks are far easier than meals. You could suggest that you join the group before or after their meal for a drink. At a meal, you're basically cemented in place from starter to dessert, without much of a choice about who you speak to. For drinks, you can more easily choose who you chat to, and leave when you feel as if it's all getting too much.

Tip 5: The lip service solution – One drink

No kissing involved – we just mean doing the bare minimum. If you never show up to drinks after work it can isolate you somewhat, but how about just staying for one drink and then making a polite retreat? It's better than nothing and here's the useful thing: it will desensitize you to office socials by making them slightly less daunting, so that anything you *are* obliged to go to doesn't build up into a mental social mountain that's impossible to climb.

Everything is easier once you're slightly familiar with it, so (figuratively speaking) a toe dipped in the water – just one drink – ain't a bad thing if you can hack it. You may even end up staying a bit longer than you thought you would and find a like-minded person who will be comforting to approach at future events.

Tip 6: The Fight Club rule

You may know the famous line from the movie *Fight Club* (1999) – 'The first rule of fight club is you don't talk about fight club'.[1] When

---

1   This is a well-known quote from the film *Fight Club* (1999), meaning to keep secret what happens within that setting.

it comes to the morning after the office social, the general principle applies here too. It doesn't mean you deny all knowledge of a social event having taken place, just that you should be careful about referring back to anything that occurred that might cause someone embarrassment or annoyance.

For instance, if you're at an event where the booze is flowing, you'll find that as your colleagues get more drunk they'll give away more about their private lives. If, after a good many drinks, they've indelicately divulged the details of a disastrous one night stand, avoid talking about it in the office when everyone is stone cold sober. It's likely they're regretting mentioning it – or might not even remember that they did!

Tip 7: How to say no

Unless you've taken a job where social events are part of your role – for instance, as an event organizer or where there's a requirement to entertain clients – nobody can force you to participate if you really don't want to and you can always politely decline. The emphasis here is on 'politely'.

The key is to avoid anyone taking it personally. As the most famous break-up line of all time goes, 'It's not you, it's me'. People may need to be reassured you're not shunning their company, just doing some sensible self-advocacy. You could, for instance, remind them of your sensory sensitivities (if you have them) and explain that a noisy bar may be fun for them but is one of Dante's circles of hell[2] for you. Or, if you have social anxiety (there it is again, that pesky S-word) and you're comfortable talking about it, you could explain that the nervous energy involved outweighs the enjoyment for you.

---

2   From Dante's famous 14th Century epic poem *The Divine Comedy*. Dante depicts hell as nine concentric circles of torment located within the Earth.

It would be lovely if, in the future, you could just say 'because autism' when somebody asks you why you don't fancy going to a social event, but unless people know a lot about you and your particular autistic experience of the world it's likely you'll have to give some form of explanation.

Tip 8: Chatting at parties
One thing to remember is that a little alcohol can make people a lot more relaxed in office socials. In this kind of environment it's easy to say something that you may later regret. To be honest, most people have done that: gone back to work on a Monday realizing that they've let slip something that they wouldn't have said in a more formal setting. Not to worry. Unless you feel it's really harmful to your job, you're best to avoid mentioning it. With any luck, everyone else will have forgotten or been too busy wondering about their own faux pas (if you've not come across that idiom, it's a French phrase meaning 'social oops!').

By the way, it's not only autistic people who suffer at office socials. It's worth knowing that many of our more introverted office workers suffer in silence, too. There should be some form of support group... Maybe we'll form the group Grounds for Reasonable Objection Against Night-time Socials (GROANS). Quite catchy, huh?

And when it comes to those who can't see what the problem is, some people may never 'get it', but that's more about them than you. It's not their fault, they just have a bad case of Social Obsessive Disorder. You should really feel sorry for the poor SODs.

CHAPTER 19

ONWARDS AND UPWARDS!

No, we're not talking here about being upgraded to one of the plusher offices upstairs (though that could happen). This chapter is to help you think about your future career goals.

Okay, it might seem a bit presumptuous to be talking about this if you're still just at the stage of applying for jobs or have only just got one, but it's a good idea to have at least some idea of your longer-term plans and aspirations.

It's a bit like planning a trip – do you want to take a coach trip to your local beach or jet off to an exotic destination with some interesting stopovers along the way? In other words, is the job you're in or applying for the one you want to stay in until you hit retirement age and somebody presents you with a nice clock? Or is it a stepping stone to something else?

As with so many decisions in life, there is no absolute right or wrong answer. If you're in a job you find satisfying and rewarding, you may not want to give it up to try something else. It can be beneficial to your self-esteem if a job is allowing you to play to your strengths and use expertise you've built up over time.

Or perhaps you just want a job that pays the bills and lets you have the space to enjoy your interests outside work or fulfil your caring responsibilities. Some people prefer a job that allows them to work relatively independently and don't apply for roles that involve managing other people. All of that is totally fine. Just because everyone around you is trying to climb the greasy pole (as advancing in your career is sometimes referred to), it doesn't mean you have to join them. All that grease. Ugh.

Knowing when it's the right time for a move

You may find yourself getting bored and frustrated, even feeling trapped, if you stay in the same role for too long or if you see yourself being overtaken by colleagues and you know you can perform at least as well as them. These may be signs you are ready for advancement.

Sometimes you would benefit most from a sideways move, either inside or outside your organization. (A 'sideways' move is when you don't get promoted but you switch roles to something new, not a way to describe 'dad dancing' at a wedding). Getting new experience at a similar level can help equip you for more responsibility later on, or just help to keep you interested in your work.

It's a good idea to seek your manager's opinion on whether and when might be the right time for a change. If you have an annual performance appraisal, this is the ideal time to get their views. In this instance, though, it's important you let them know why you're considering a move. You don't want them to think you're unhappy in your current role or not committed to it.

If you don't explain your motivation, your manager may make their own assumptions, and you don't want to risk damaging your working relationship. You might want to start off, therefore, by reassuring them that you enjoy your current role (assuming you do – you don't have to lie) but would welcome their input on how you might further develop your experience.

It might be that you can't wait to get away from your current manager and you routinely fantasize about putting duct tape across their mouth every time they speak to you. But you can't tell them that, sorry. Both Debby and Maura have had some great managers and some not so good ones, but have learnt something from every person they've worked for – even if it's just that it's not a good idea to dump all of your work onto somebody then perch on the end of their desk for hours on end thereby preventing them from getting on with it. Do not do that...

What might be holding you back?

If you've grown up undiagnosed, misdiagnosed or just plain misunderstood, you may have a little voice in the back of your head that tells you you're not good enough. It's a lie. Seek out other voices and objective evidence about the quality of your work and your abilities instead.

Lots of people take the approach of 'fake it until you make it'. Just because you don't naturally have an abundance of self-confidence, it shouldn't stop you from progressing in your chosen career. Most people have self-doubt to some degree.

We've been talking about perfectionism a few times in this book and with good reason – it's a very common trait among autistic people. It can have advantages, such as providing the impetus to excel at something, but can be like Kryptonite[1] as well. If you don't believe you can do something absolutely perfectly, you may not even want to try. The thing to remember is that nobody is 100% good at 100% of things 100% of the time. Not even Superman. Everyone will have a learning curve in a new role and you will not be expected to know everything at once.

---

1   Kryptonite is a fictional material that appears in Superman stories published by DC Comics. It is from Superman's home planet Krypton and is deadly to people who come from the planet.

Fear of change might be another factor. The great unknown. The prospect of working with different people, in a different environment, with different responsibilities. It could all seem quite overwhelming. But bear in mind few decisions in life are completely final and if it doesn't work out, you can usually move on to something else at some point. And if you pass up a good opportunity, you may find yourself regretting that decision much more.

At the other extreme, some people move around way too much. It's usually a case of FOMO (fear of missing out), being too quick to burn their bridges (sever links) with other people or such a lack of confidence in their abilities that they try to get out before the balls start dropping (another phrase for making mistakes). The problem with not staying in any particular role for a decent amount of time is that it will make it harder for you to have anything to show for your efforts. If you want to advance, you want to be in a position to demonstrate solid achievements, which is difficult to do if your CV shows you flit about between jobs like an over-active butterfly. Most employers see past performance as the best indicator of future potential, and want evidence of your ability to deliver.

Shift happens

Always remember, your career plan does not have to be fixed as though it's been carved in stone (though if you were able to do that, it would be quite impressive). 'Life is what happens to you while you're busy making other plans', as the late great John Lennon famously said and tragically proved (Lennon & Ono, 1980). A plan needs to be flexible so you can update it whenever the need arises. You might find a great opportunity you hadn't even thought about before, your interests could move on or there could be changes in your personal circumstances.

Maura is quite relieved now she didn't stick to the career choices she made when she was eight years old, which were either ballerina or trapeze artist. (*Yeh?* says Debby. *Well I wanted to be a princess with three dogs on leads. Followed by an archaeologist because I found a piece of broken pipe in my garden.*)

In the end, your quality of life is what is most important. It may take some effort to find that sweet spot between feeling comfortable in a role and experiencing enough of a challenge for it to hold your interest. But it will be worth it.

However you spend your working life, know that we're with you (in spirit) all the way! You're not in the workplace to tread a path for neurodivergent people to follow, nor are you there to create tolerance and understanding – you're there because you deserve to be fulfilled and because others benefit from your skills and knowledge. The more autistic people there are in offices, the more office staff will learn to be flexible enough to accommodate them.

So go for it! And good luck!

CHAPTER 20

YOUR OFFICE—
ENGLISH, ENGLISH—
OFFICE DICTIONARY

You can consider this book finished. However, here's an extra reference chapter to dip into for your own amusement and we hope you'll find it useful. And it lets us have an even number of chapters that is also a multiple of five. (*Sweet* – Maura.)

Here, as a continuation of the subject we started in Chapter 5, you'll find all manner of phrases and idioms used in an office environment. Use the blank page after the chapter to add your own if you like (if this isn't a library book, that is. Don't be naughty).

Phrases for feeling over-worked

These get their own section since there are a lot of them, usually uttered by people who'd rather spend 20 minutes telling you how busy they are than actually do any flippin' work.

I've got too much on my plate!

Usually having lots on your plate is a good thing, but in terms of work, 'too much on your plate' or 'enough on your plate' means you're at your limit. Saying 'I'm really stretched' doesn't imply that someone has turned into a bendy fidget toy (shame), but is another phrase for being at the limit of what they can comfortably achieve.

I'm snowed under
You can have a lot on your plate, be stretched or snowed under. The choice is yours. They all mean you have too much work on.

I'm burning the candle at both ends!
Working to exhaustion, usually early morning till late at night.

No peace (or rest) for the wicked!
Mildly amusing biblical term implying that the person is in some way sinful and, therefore, obliged to work all the time as punishment. People say it when they have to get on with work having taken a small break, maybe to chat.

Overworked and underpaid!
Sometimes when you ask someone from another company or department how they are, this is their standard 'amusing' response. It isn't a serious complaint, although there might be an element of truth there. A decent response is 'Join the club!' which means 'Yes, we all experience the same problem'.

General office chat phrases

We have a word count to stick to so we can't cover absolutely everything, but these should give you a decent enough flavour.

I need to get you up to speed...
I need to bring you up-to-date or teach you. For example, I'll get you up to speed on this new system.

I'd like to reach out to you...

Urghh. We hate this one. 'Reach out' just means someone would like to communicate with you, but doesn't specify how. They aren't defining whether it would be by post, phone, e-mail, or face-to-face. Usually it's in an opening e-mail from someone you haven't met before, and you choose the method of contact. Or, to ignore them entirely if they're just trying to sell you something...

I just want to give you the heads up...

I'd like to give you advance warning. Thus, your head could do with being up to receive this information, rather than your head not really listening much and being bowed over whatever's more interesting, like Tik Tok.

S/he hasn't got a leg to stand on or No leg to stand on

Not a factual comment. Means that someone does not have the remotest chance of winning an argument because of points that they have made which are untrue or weak.

Every cloud...

Short for 'every cloud has a silver lining'. Means there is one benefit to the bad news. For example, 'The conference is boring as heck, but they do a lovely free lunch. So, every cloud...'

One thing worth knowing: sometimes people use 'every cloud...' sarcastically. So, if the drawback or 'cloud' is MASSIVE but the benefit or 'silver lining' is REALLY TINY in comparison, people may say 'every cloud...' as a joke. For example, 'Global warming means it's now hot enough to grow vine trees in the south of England and so we'll finally get some decent wine. So, every cloud...'

In this case we don't seriously mean that there is a silver lining, but just that the benefit is really pathetic, and it's worth pointing out just how pathetic this is with a joke. This might not be your idea of a solid joke, but people do use it.

They're not pulling their weight
They aren't putting in their share of effort.

They're punching above their weight
A boxing metaphor, meaning someone is performing above their level.

A busman's holiday
Means you are giving advice or doing work in your leisure time which is the same as the work you do for a living. For example, 'Bit of a busman's holiday for you, isn't it?' in which case avoid replying with 'I cannot drive a bus'. Or, do that for a joke and watch how everyone gets nervous about whether the literal thinker minds them laughing.

You want to try...
In different areas 'You want to' means different things. Some people say 'You want to try doing it this way...' as a genuine suggestion, meaning 'I'd recommend you try this'. At other times, it can be used sarcastically, especially when someone is saying their situation is worse than yours. 'You think that's bad? You want to try working for Peter Pitts!' In this example, you most definitely wouldn't want to try working for Peter Pitts. If someone's eyebrows move up when they say it and they're grinning, it's probably being used sarcastically.

Play your trump card or Mine trumps that!
In some areas of the UK, a 'trump' means breaking wind. Whereas in the US, it's a former President. If you say you're playing your trump card, or something 'trumps' another thing (verb), it is a card-playing metaphor. A trump card is a playing card that wins over all others.

Head office is on the phone

Or, they might use a place name where another office is based, like 'London is on the phone'. This sounds distinctly impossible. All they mean is 'Someone from head office has called...'

Phrases to describe people and their positions

We're not talking about yoga positions or political standpoints here, just reflecting the fact that people in offices can be quite grade conscious.

Head honcho

Leader.

Top brass

Leadership – usually more than one person.

Number 2

This is not a poo although sometimes this phrase is used to mean it. This means 'second in command' or deputy. You might find the combination of the two meanings gets a laugh.

'He's the Number 2 there, I believe...'
'Yes, I've heard he is a bit of a Number 2'.

Those at the coal face

At the coal face doesn't literally mean they're down a coal mine you'll be pleased to hear. It's a phrase used to describe people who have face-to-face contact with customers or service users, or do the daily, less glamorous work of the organization.

Usually, they are the lower paid among office workers who ensure that the organization keeps running.

In an ivory tower

Saying a manager lives in an ivory tower is not a compliment. It means that they are in an isolated and privileged position, and not in touch with the everyday people working at the 'coal face'. Plus, ivory towers don't have disability adaptations so no one is going to reach them without a hike up some stairs. (Yes, we are being sarcastic.) Apologies to lighthouse workers, who despite working in ivory-coloured towers are not in a privileged position at all and do a great job. When they're there in person. Most of it is automated these days. Have we gone off the point, here? Who thought of this phrase, anyway?

Jobsworth

Insulting term for people who insist on rules being followed, even when it defies common sense. They won't put themselves out for others and show no flexibility at all. They're the type of person who would say 'It's more than my job's worth to let you do that!'

Often they'll point out when you haven't filled in a form adequately in order for it to be 'signed off' or 'rubber stamped', which means 'given the okay'. If you're in an administrative role, a cheerful manner when giving people boring paperwork goes a very long way, as does an apology if the boring paperwork has to be altered and amended. People who love paperwork are rather rare.

Pen pusher

This term gets used for people who have to do a lot of dull and repetitive paperwork, probably because they work for a jobsworth. It's not a complimentary thing to call someone, even if it's the type of job they have to do.

Bean counter

People who are 'bean counters' or 'hold the purse strings' work on the company's finances. If you describe someone as a 'bean counter', it's insulting; you're implying that they think more about the cost of something than its actual importance. In some ways, this is very unfair to accountants, whose job is to look after finances. They wouldn't be great at it if they told everyone to spend, spend, spend.

Many of these terms are used by people who never meet the 'bean counter' or the 'pen pusher' in question, and so don't really see things from another person's point of view.

Just tell them to have a bit of empathy and then grin as much as you like for smashing another misconception about autistic people.

If you're trying to tell someone that you can't say yes to something because it's someone else who makes the financial decision on it, you might say: 'It's not me who holds the purse strings, I'm afraid'.

This just means, I don't make the financial decisions round here. 'Purse strings' is a 16th-century idiom which refers to when people kept coins in a bag, rather than a wallet. Eat your heart out, Sandi Toksvig.[1]

Whilst we're on the subject of money, if someone asks you for a 'ballpark figure' they are asking you for an estimate on how much something might cost.

Too many cooks...

This refers to the phrase 'too many cooks spoil the broth' and is often shortened in conversation. Too many managers and not enough workers.

Frequent flyer

Someone who often travels by plane. However, it also gets used to describe someone who's a bit of a nuisance, such as somebody who's constantly contacting their doctor even though there's nothing much wrong with them.

---

1 Danish-British comedian who now hosts the spectacularly obscure knowledge quiz show QI, shown on British TV.

High flyer
Someone who has ambitions for a top job – or already occupies a senior role.

Part-timer
Can be used literally to mean a person who works part-time, but as an idiom it's also a term to make (usually gentle) fun of someone who frequently arrives late or goes home early. You don't need to be upset if someone uses it on you if you have to leave early. 'See you tomorrow, part-timer!'

If they're smiling, they're probably just kidding around and not really accusing you of lacking dedication, though we don't recommend using it yourself since it could be seen as implying part-time workers are less committed.

Guinea pig
Guinea pig is a term for a person trialling something new. So, if someone says 'I'll be a guinea pig, if you like' they are offering to test out something, not live in a cage and drink from an upside-down water bottle.

Moonlighter
Someone who also has another job, usually a secret one. How anyone has the energy for more than one job is beyond us.

Phrases regarding time

Office workers use a lot of these too, which makes sense since most are paid for doing a certain number of hours.

Early doors
First thing in the morning.

I'm clocking off or Knocking off
Old factory term, means I'm going home now. By the way, knocking off should generally be avoided these days, as it also means 'having sex with...' as in 'I heard he's knocking off his assistant...'

This does not mean they're both going home early. Although they probably will be.

Close of play
Sporting term for the end of the working day. If someone wants it 'on my desk by close of play' it means they want to see something by the end of the day.

Beer o' clock
Drinks after work.

Hump day
Wednesday. The suggestion is that once you've gotten over Wednesday (or the 'hump' in the week) the weekend is closer – wahay!

Thursday is the new Friday
For people who go out after work on a Thursday. Strange beings with lots of social energy.

The long weekend
Used to really confuse us. You can't stretch Saturday or Sunday. However, when Monday is a bank holiday, for instance, in effect you do experience a longer weekend.

It's a short week next week!
Hello? Next week is no shorter than any other. It means that it's a shorter working week, because of a bank holiday or public holiday.

The working week
Refers to Monday to Friday.

Phrases used in teamwork

It still bugs us there's no 'we' in team, especially since 'teamwork' is an anagram of 'me at work'. But hey.

Put it to me in Mickey Mouse terms
Explain it simply. Usually if you're tech-savvy, you get asked to explain things without jargon to non-technical colleagues. (Again, no disrespect to the mouse intended.)

Been there, got the T-shirt!
I've had that experience, too. Similar to 'Join the club!'

I need a sounding board
Don't look around the room for a plank of wood. A sounding board is someone who can objectively listen to thoughts and give their views.

Hold that thought!
Yeh, not literally. Just pause what you are saying. Someone has been interrupted whilst listening to you but they will be listening to you again in a very short while. Stay there and wait.

That's our bread and butter
That's the basics of what we do – usually what brings in the most income, even if it's not very glamorous or new.

Stand ups
What a great company, they've asked you to come to a stand up at 9am! Before you look forward to listening to Peter Kay[2] or Hannah

---

2   Entertaining comedian from the North of England known for great observational humour. We particularly like it when he describes guests on the dancefloor at weddings.

Gadsby,[3] we have to warn you that a 'stand up' in office-speak is far more boring. These are short meetings of around 15 minutes, usually regular ones. The idea is that people stand for the meeting to encourage keeping it short and succinct. Which isn't a bad idea if you don't much like meetings (WHO DOES?) but should be paired with the phrase 'sit downs' for longer meetings. It isn't, unless you're in the USA. Few things are logical in the office world.

Kill two birds

Short for the phrase 'Kill two birds with one stone'. To do one thing that has two benefits to it. Not exactly what we'd call a positive analogy, as most of us like to feed our feathery friends and not go around chucking stones at them.

There's more than one way to skin a cat

Who thought of that one? Like you were even thinking about doing this – huh?! As we're typing, Maura's cat Baz and Debby's cat Ernie are hiding under their respective tables. It means there's more than one way to do things. It's possibly our least favourite phrase EVER.

Keep your foot to the pedal/to the floor

Keep going at a fast pace – driving metaphor.

My bad

This means 'that's my misunderstanding, sorry' (or 'my fault'). Terrible, isn't it?

Low-hanging fruit

The most easily achieved bit of a task. So, the task is being compared with a fruit tree where some of the lower fruit are easier to pick. For example, 'Well, let's not waste too much time and go for the low-hanging fruit first'.

---

3   Australian autistic comedian.

Take the line/path of least resistance
Taking the easiest path. It's sometimes used in situations where the quickest route isn't necessarily the best, or even the right thing to do.

Iron out the creases
Solve any final problems.

Phrases to describe taking a risk

Out on a limb
Taking a risk, and on your own. Someone who is 'out on a limb' is like they're on a single branch of a tree that's not well supported. For example, 'I'm going out on a limb with this idea, but I think it might work!'

You can't make an omelette without breaking eggs
There might be some drawbacks along the way to get a good outcome.

Neck on the block or Sticking your neck out
A charming hark back to the old days when justice meant that people got their heads chopped off. If you are sticking your neck out you are taking a risk; if your neck is on the block, you're doing something that means you could be in big, big trouble if it goes pear-shaped. And just in case you're wondering...

Phrases for when things go wrong

We quite like some of these, since they soften the blow a bit when there's a problem.

Sticky wicket
This is yet another of those trusty cricket metaphors, used to describe something difficult or tricky.

Pear-shaped

It's not very fair on pears, but apples and peaches tend to be used as metaphors for everything going well. 'It's all apple pie', for instance, means everything is perfectly in order. And if 'everything's just peachy' it's a good thing.

Pear-shaped, by contrast, means that everything is going wrong.

Swimming against the tide

Going in a different direction and facing resistance.

Going against the grain

A woodwork term for going in a different direction and facing resistance. All good woodworkers know that you can only plane a piece of wood in one direction. Thank you, Mr Woodhouse, for teaching Debby woodwork when she was 13 so that she could finally share this insight. She made a lovely wooden mask that scared the bejaysus out of anyone coming to the house. Still, er, a useful lesson for life. And pretty handy if you don't want people to come to your house – she's taking orders on Etsy.[4]

It's a minefield

There are a lot of potential problems to negotiate, here. Step the wrong way and it could be bad news.

On the back foot

Another sporting metaphor. If you say you've caught someone 'on the back foot', you've got them at a disadvantage. If you're the one on the back foot, you've been outmanoeuvred.

Knocked for six

Yet another sporting metaphor. This means something has hit you hard, usually bad news.

---

4   An online company that specializes in handmade and vintage stuff.

'He's resigned? That's knocked me for six'.

Phrases used in ideas or problem-solving meetings

Strap yourself in there, buckaroo – these types of meetings spawn turbo-charged idioms, and plenty of them!

Pencil it in

No pencils required. It means this is a rough or tentative plan and is subject to change if required. It's usually used for diary dates that might be changed.

Brainstorming

Everyone throwing their thoughts out there, with the basic premise that being plunged into a sea of group creativity will eventually amount to finding one good idea. If you've ever watched *The Apprentice*,[5] you'll know that brainstorming isn't often all it's cracked up to be.

Brainstorming is sometimes referred to as a 'thought shower' as it may be considered more respectful towards those who have epilepsy.

Teaching you to suck eggs or Teaching Grandma to suck eggs

This is one of the most bizarre idioms in the English language. Why would you need to be taught such a thing? It means teaching you how to do something you're already very capable of doing. Usually it can be translated as 'I don't want to tell you how to do something when you already know...'

---

5   Business-style reality TV game show in which contestants work in two teams, quite often dreaming up bad product ideas with even worse marketing. If their team loses, contestants usually spend quite a long time at the end of the show going on about why this wasn't their idea personally so that they don't get sacked. It's all very stressful.

Blue sky thinking
No limits on ideas. Free as a bird, your mind doesn't have to worry about practicalities just yet.

Run it up the flagpole
Test out an idea, as if it is a flag being hoisted. Beautiful crap if ever we saw it.

No cheese down that tunnel
Beautiful crap for 'There's nothing to be gained by following that line of thought'.

Thinking outside the box
Being imaginative and dreaming up new and radical solutions. The word 'box' suggests that this thinking has been confined to current, narrow ideas.

Green light
The go-ahead to proceed with something. For example, 'Head office has given us the green light on that project'.

Pull the plug on...
The opposite of the 'green light' – this project has been stopped.

Light bulb moment
The moment in which inspiration strikes.

Rough around the edges
A piece of work is a basic version and needs refining.

Playing devil's advocate
This means putting forward a point of view that you don't necessarily think to be correct, but you feel is necessary to consider. So, you're pretending to be championing the opposite argument,

just for the sake of the group considering it. For example, 'Playing devil's advocate here, what if people respond badly to the last line of that press release?' This means you don't really feel that people will respond badly, but it's something that ought to be considered.

We need their buy-in
We need their agreement or approval.

Lean in
You may be forgiven for thinking that someone who offers to 'lean in' isn't being especially helpful and might want to just nosey over what you're doing on the computer. However, 'I'm happy to lean in on that matter' basically means to lend help or expertise and assist.

Be thrown a curve ball
An unexpected problem being thrown your way.

Kicking it into the long grass
Putting off a decision, usually until it's someone else's problem.

Kicking the can down the road
Putting off a decision, usually until it's someone else's problem.

Putting it on ice or Putting it on the back burner
Confusingly, whether you put it on something hot or cold, it means the same. Both mean leaving an idea for a while, or putting it at a lower priority.

Rear-view mirror thinking
Focusing on what's already happened.

Are we on the same page?
Are we in agreement?

Red tape

Rules and regulations that get in the way of what you're trying to achieve.

My hands are tied

Are they? I didn't notice... Nope, they are tied in a figurative sense. This means someone is prevented from making a decision because of rules, regulations or a higher authority. They're saying nope, I can't help you, because that's not my decision to make. It's sometimes very tempting to say 'Well untie them, then'.

Other phrases that we can't find a heading for

Non-starter

Not a great idea.

Wet signature

An actual signed signature with an actual pen.

Digital signature

Something that you sign digitally by typing your name at the right place on a form, and e-mailing it back.

In the return post

Generally means it's been returned immediately in the post.

Drop me a line

Nope, they're not taking you fishing. They mean send me a note (usually digitally these days).

YOUR STAFF BONUS: OFFICE TYPES – CAN YOU SPOT THEM?

Every office has them, certain difficult types. We've made a list of the types of people we've worked with. Give yourself a point whenever you spot one yourself.

Office type	What they're like
The albatross	A mood hoover with more baggage than a left luggage storeroom
The ant	Hardworking, team player
The bee	Busy, productive and quite nice, provided you're not a threat
The blackbird	Starts early but is entirely useless after lunch
The butterfly	Flits around picking up news and gossip
The cockroach	Adaptable enough to survive any situation but can leave a bit of a stink
The cricket	Rarely shuts up
The crow	Keeps themselves to themselves and occasionally looks up if there's a fire or something
The eagle	High flying visionary at the top of the food chain who's both impressive and intimidating

cont.

Office type	What they're like
The hen	Mothers everyone and is a supplier of spare hankies, postage stamps and home-baked treats
The macaw	Loud, colourful and enjoys being the centre of attention
The magpie	Will nick your ideas as well as your stapler
The owl	Experienced, respected and worth listening to
The parrot	Agrees with everyone to their face
The peacock	Loves the glory and will show off what they've done to anyone and everyone. If you've got a magpie who is also a peacock, avoid. If they're your boss, bad luck
The seagull	Can always be relied upon to poo on you from a great height
The sparrow	Shy and reserved, quietly reliable
The vulture	Revels in the office gossip
The wasp	Pretends to be your friend then stings you in the arse when there's something to be gained
The woodpecker	Tends to go on a bit and is rather demanding, to the point where you have a headache

REFERENCES

Czarska, A. (dir. and writer) (2021) *Mildly different*. Sticky Tape Productions. Streamed on 29 August 2023 at www.stickytapefilms.com/mildlydifferent

Johnson, Boris (2021) 'The crocus of hope is poking through the frost'. Press conference, February 22 2021. London, Downing Street.

Lennon, J. & Ono, Y. (1980) Beautiful boy. *Double Fantasy* [album]. Geffen Records.

Milton, D. (2012) On the ontological status of autism: The 'double empathy problem'. *Disability and Society*, 27(6), 883–887.

UK Government (1995) *Disability Discrimination Act 1995*. Accessed on 29 August 2023 at www.legislation.gov.uk/ukpga/1995/50/contents

UK Government (2010) *Equality Act 2010*. Accessed on 29 August 2023 at www.legislation.gov.uk/ukpga/2010/15/contents

Wikipedia (2023) Justin Bieber. Accessed on 5 September 2023 at www.wikipedia.org

FURTHER READING

The Equality Commission (2022) *In employment – workplace adjustments*. The Equality Commission. Accessed on 28 August 2023 at www. equalityhumanrights.com/en/multipage-guide/employment-workplace-adjustments (relevant to England, Scotland and Wales).

The Equality and Human Rights Commission (2019) *Reasonable adjustments in practice: Covering England, Wales and Scotland*. The Equality Commission. Accessed on 28 August 2023 at www.equalityhumanrights.com

The Equality Commission for Northern Ireland (ECNI) (n.d.) *The reasonable adjustment duty and the disability discrimination act: Covering Northern Ireland*. ECNI. Accessed on 28 August 2023 at www.equalityni.org/ReasonableAdjustments

Leggett, C. (2016) *Top autism tips: Employment – recruitment and interviews*. National Autistic Society. Accessed on 28 August 2023 at www.autism.org.uk/ advice-and-guidance/professional-practice/recruitment-interviews

Leggett, C. (2016) *Top 5 autism tips – employment: Disclosing your diagnosis*. National Autistic Society. Accessed on 28 August 2023 at www.autism.org.uk/ advice-and-guidance/professional-practice/disclosing-employment

National Autistic Society (2020) *Employing autistic people – a guide for employers*. National Autistic Society. Accessed on 28 August 2023 at www.autism.org. uk/advice-and-guidance/topics/employment/employing-autistic-people/ employers (As well as plenty of great guidance within the NAS itself, this section also has lots of useful links – including one to its own bespoke consultancy service for UK employers).

National Autistic Society (2020) *Support at work – a guide for autistic people*. National Autistic Society. Accessed on 28 August 2023 at www.autism.org.uk/ advice-and-guidance/topics/employment/support-at-work/autistic-adults (Includes advice on workplace bullying).

Swiatek, E. (2016) *Top autism tips: Employment – reasonable adjustments*. National Autistic Society. Accessed on 28 August 2023 at www.autism.org.uk/advice-and-guidance/professional-practice/employment-adjustments-tips

US Department of Labor (n.d.) *Job accommodations*. US Department of Labor. Accessed on 28 August 2023 at www.dol.gov/general/topic/disability/jobaccommodations

SUPPORT FOR YOU IN THE WORKPLACE

ACAS is an independent organization that receives government funding in the UK, gives employees and employers free, impartial advice on workplace rights, rules and best practice. They have a helpline that is open during the week and also offer training and help to resolve disputes. www.acas.org.uk. For information on constructive dismissal go to www.acas.org.uk/dismissals/constructive-dismissal

The Citizens Advice Bureau (UK) has advice about planning how to ask for adjustments. Search *'reasonable adjustments'* at www.citizensadvice.org.uk. The same organization has advice for harassment at work at www.citizensadvice.org.uk/work/discrimination-at-work/discrimination-at-work/checking-if-its-discrimination/if-youre-being-harassed-or-bullied-at-work

The Curly Hair Project at https://thegirlwiththecurlyhair.co.uk is an organization founded by autistic author Alis Rowe to help autistic people and those around them to understand each other with the use of animated films, stories, comic strips and diagrams. At the site you can access training, e-courses and other resources.

The Disability Law Service is where you can check your rights to reasonable adjustments and what sorts you're entitled to using Work Rights, the Disability Law Service's digital advice pathway, at https://dls.org.uk/workrights. This organization can also help advise you when it comes to discrimination in employment, harassment or unfair and wrongful dismissal.

EASS (Equality Advisory Support Service) has a helpline for UK employees who have experienced discrimination. They can help you to resolve the complaint informally. At www.equalityadvisoryservice.com you'll find access to a helpline (freephone telephone 0808 800 0082 – accurate on 29 August 2023) and live chat. EASS can also find a mediator to help you reach agreement over any disputes at work and can advise you on help if you have a learning disability.

The National Autistic Society runs an Understanding Autism in the Workplace training course for employers, as well as a specialist consultancy service for them. www.autism.org.uk/what-we-do/professional-development/training-and-conferences/employment/understanding-autism-in-the-workplace. The National Autistic Society also has an area of its website dedicated to advising you on bullying at work. For more information look up www.autism.org.uk/advice-and-guidance/topics/employment/support-at-work/autistic-adults

Scope (England and Wales) has a Support to Work programme you can apply for at www.scope.org.uk/employment-services/support-to-work. You can also look up their disability employment providers at www.scope.org.uk/advice-and-support/disability-friendly-employers

The Specialisterne Foundation is an international organization, founded in Denmark, with offices in a number of countries worldwide and has as its goal to create one million careers for autistic people. With autistic people and employers, they create solutions that reduce the barriers for autistic people to be part of communities, and to enjoy careers. https://specialisterne.com